Coloring is not only a fun activity, but also a powerful way to relieve stress and calm the mind.

As you immerse yourself in the images in this book, allow yourself to relax, breathe deeply, and focus on the present moment.

May this book be more than just a set of coloring pages, but rather a haven for your soul, where you can find peace and serenity whenever you need it.

So, grab your colored pencils, unleash your imagination and embark on this journey of self-discovery and well-being.

This Book Belongs to:

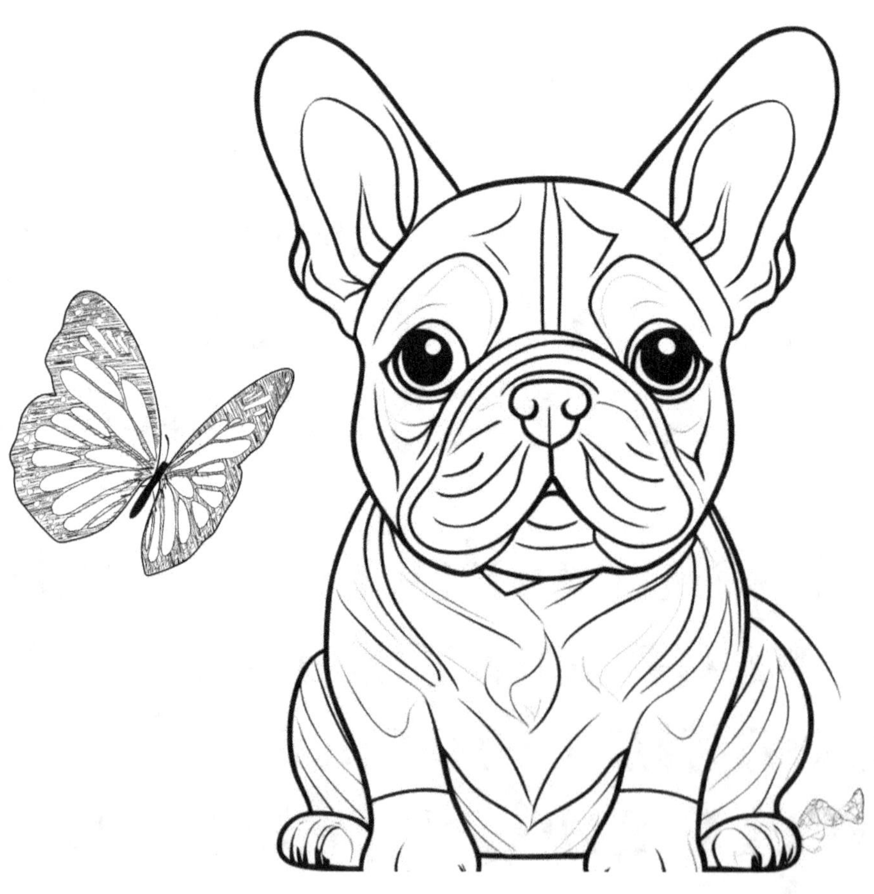

ALL RIGHTS RESERVED©
2024

No part of this publication may be reproduced, distributed, or transmitted in any form or by any means, including photocopying, recording, or other electronic or mechanical methods, without the prior written permission of the publisher, except for brief quotations incorporated in critical reviews and other specific noncommercial uses. Any unauthorized replica of this work is prohibited.

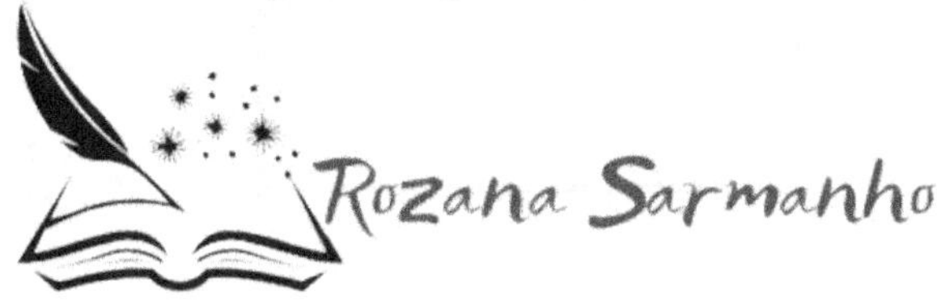

Test Color Page

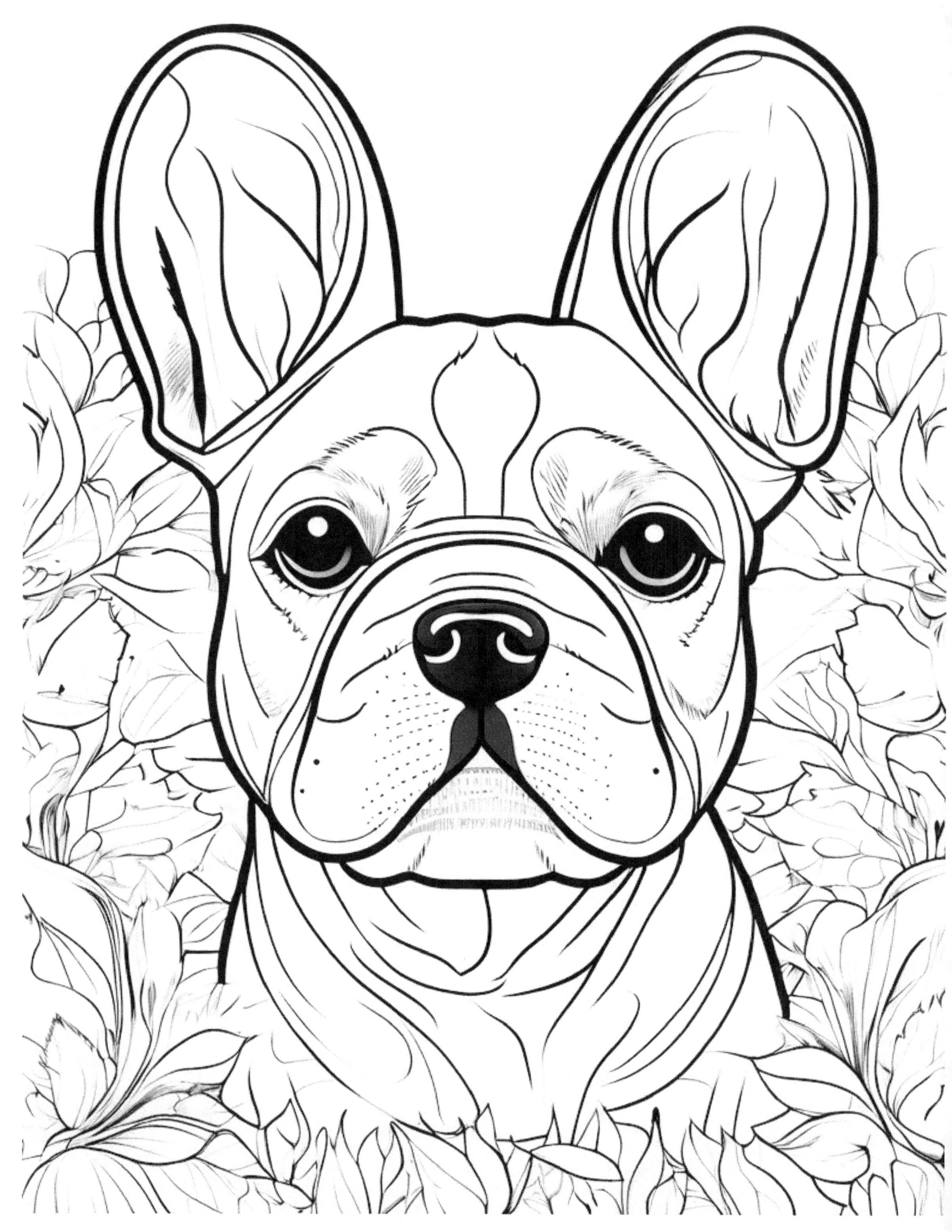

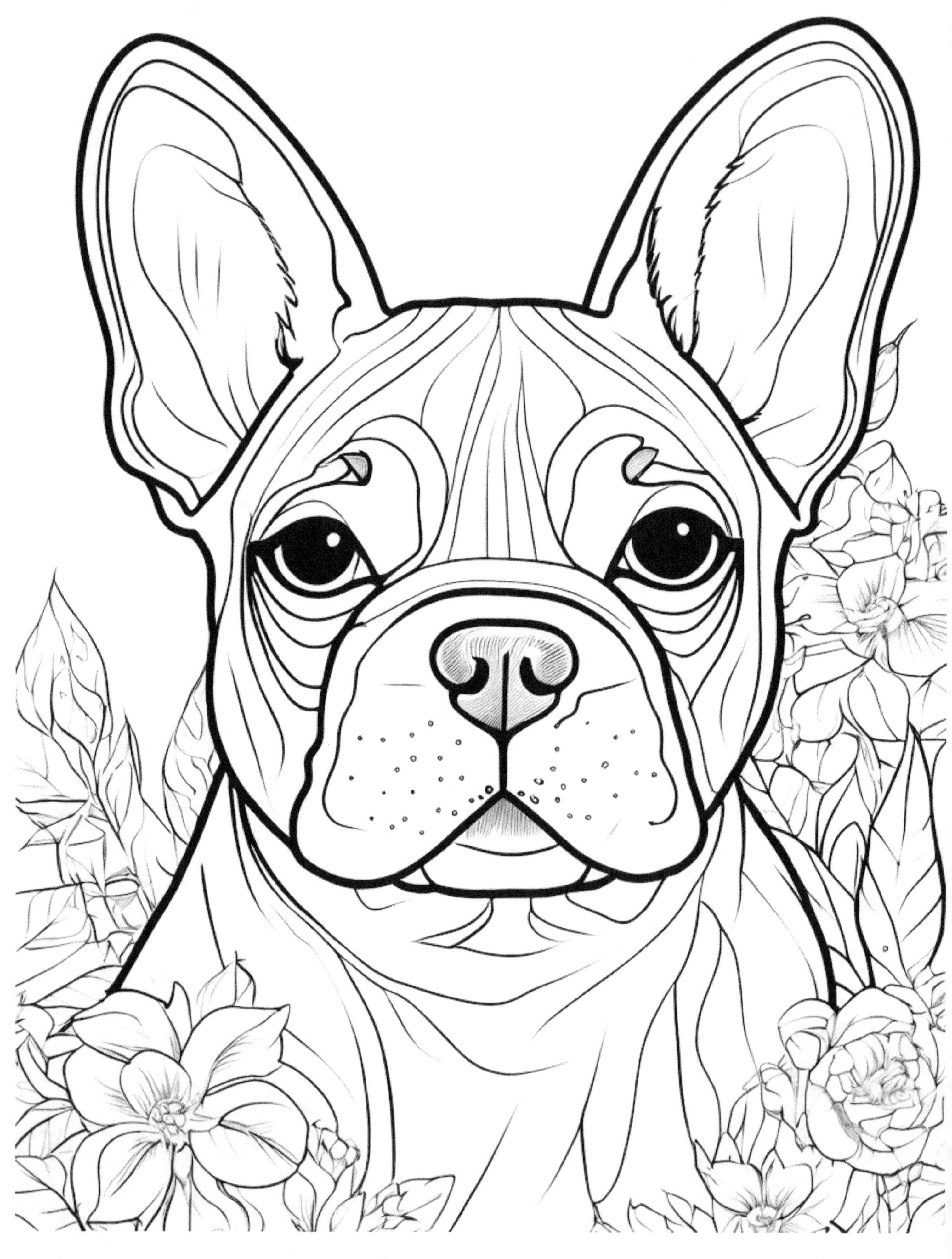

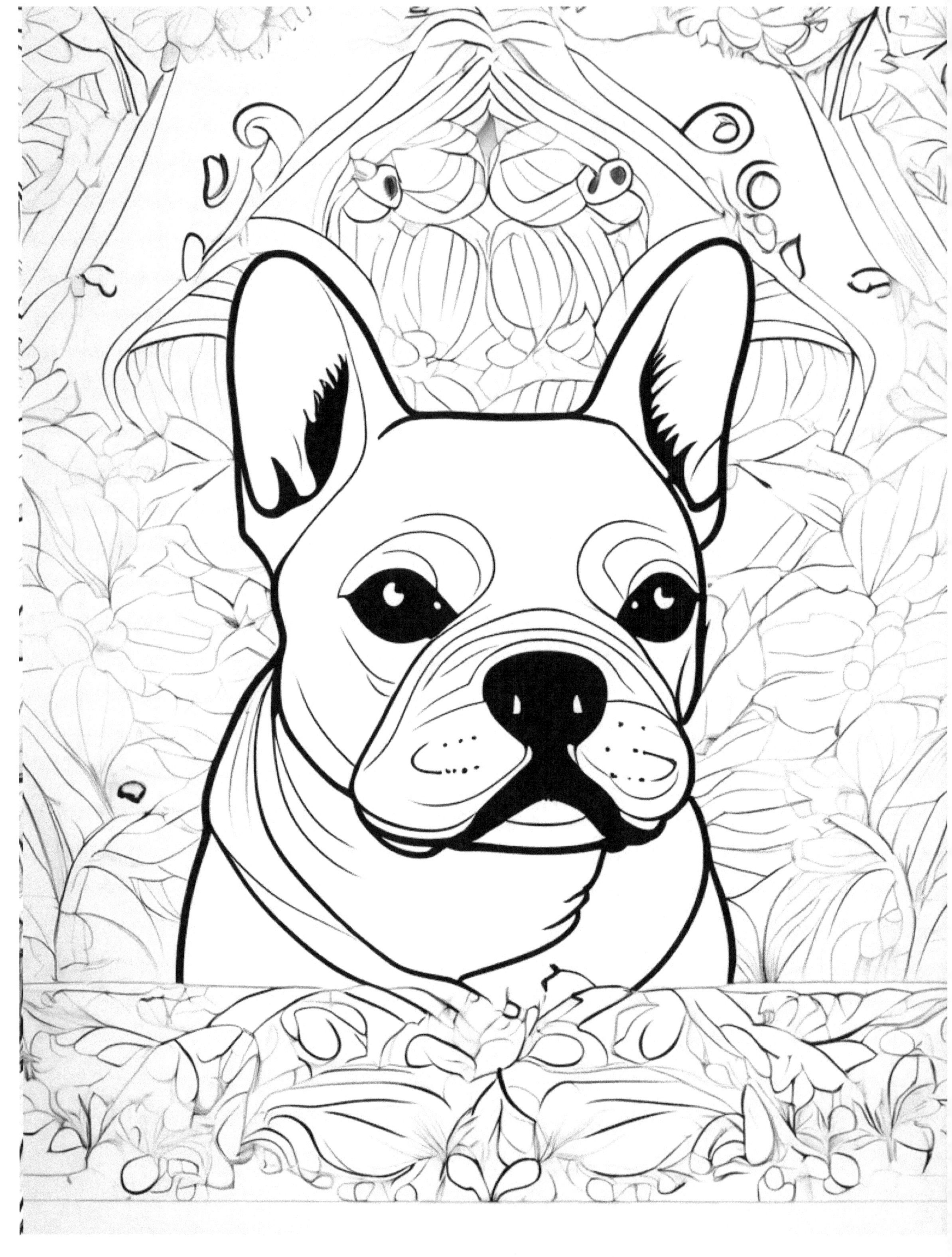

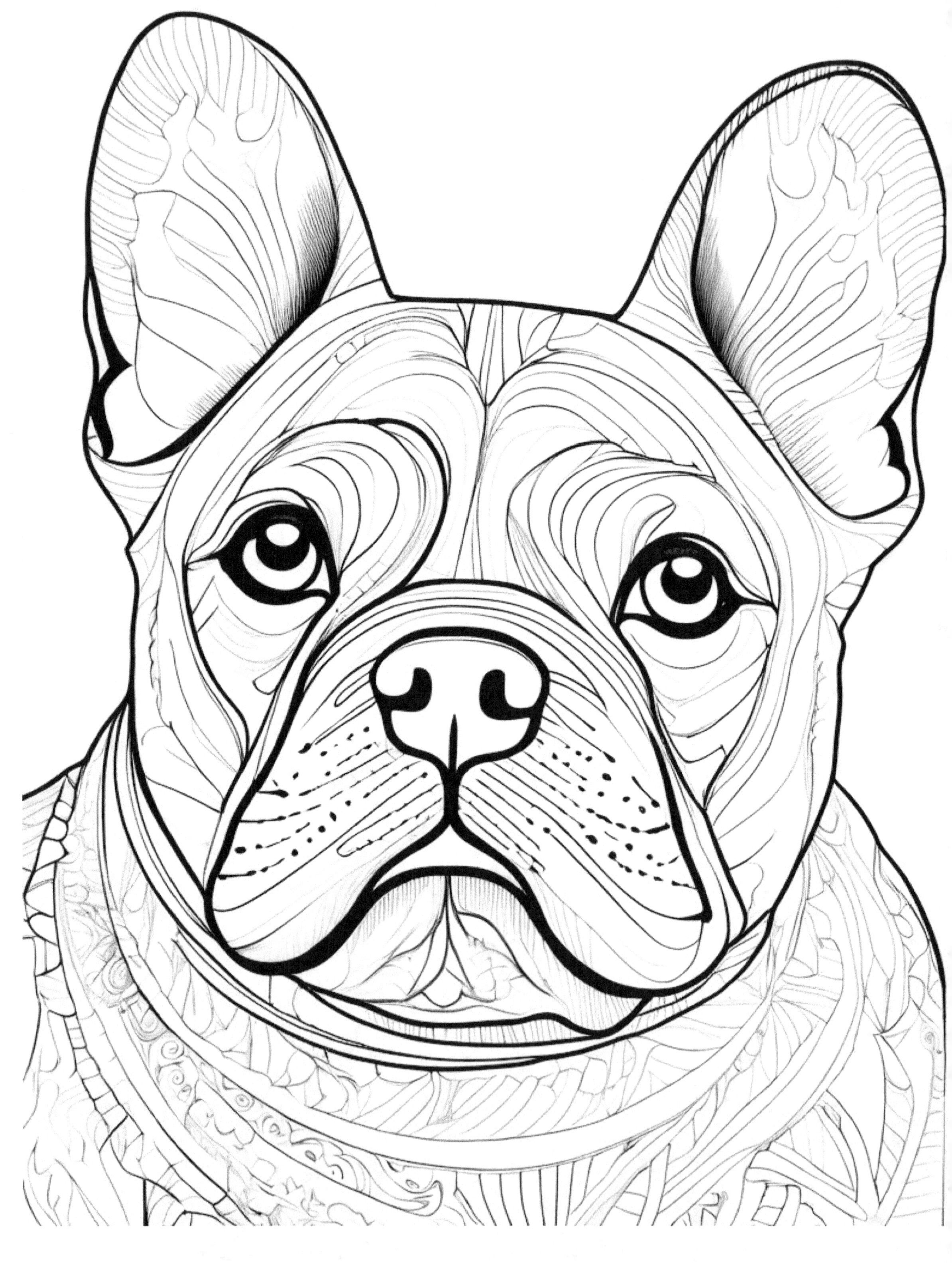

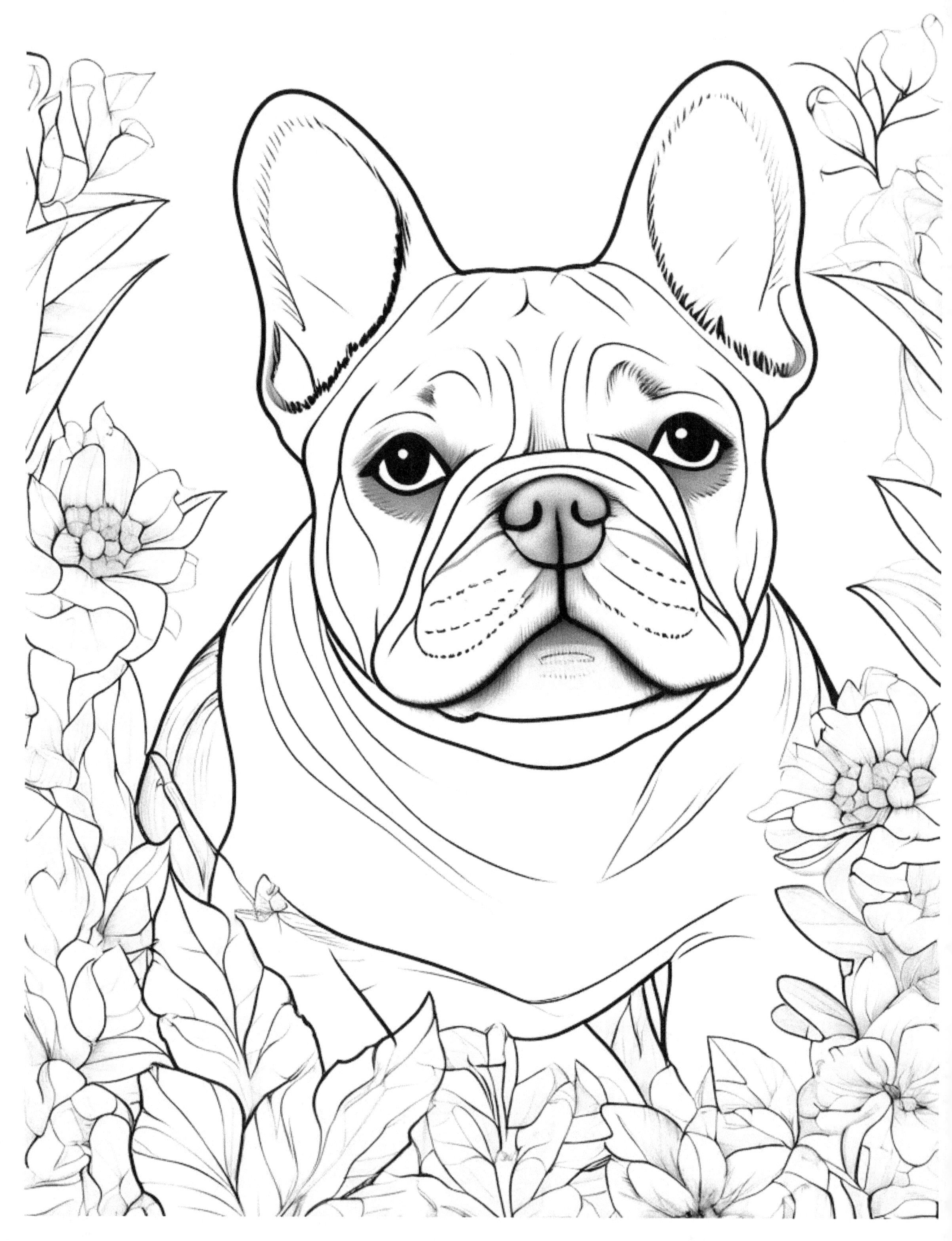

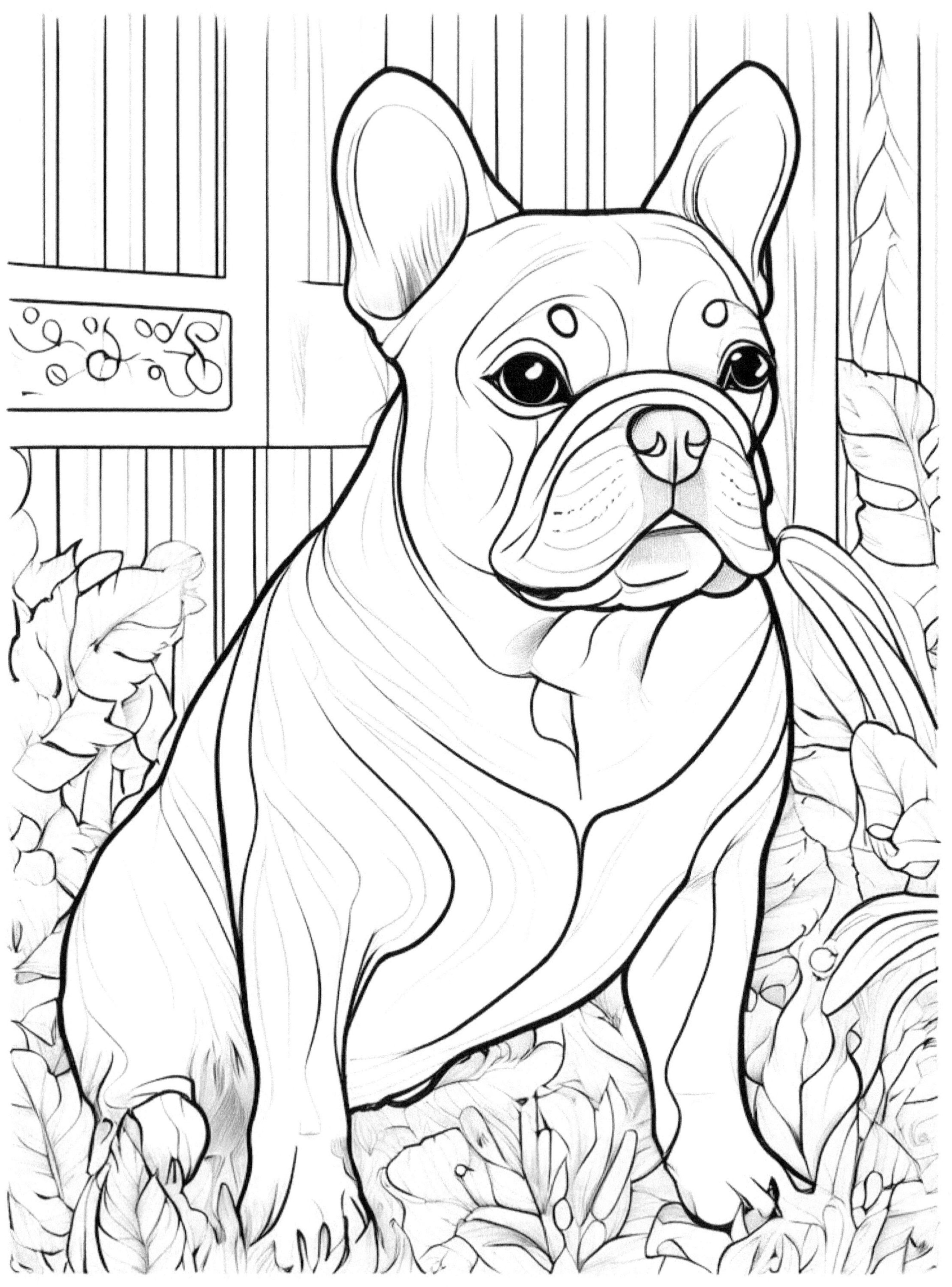

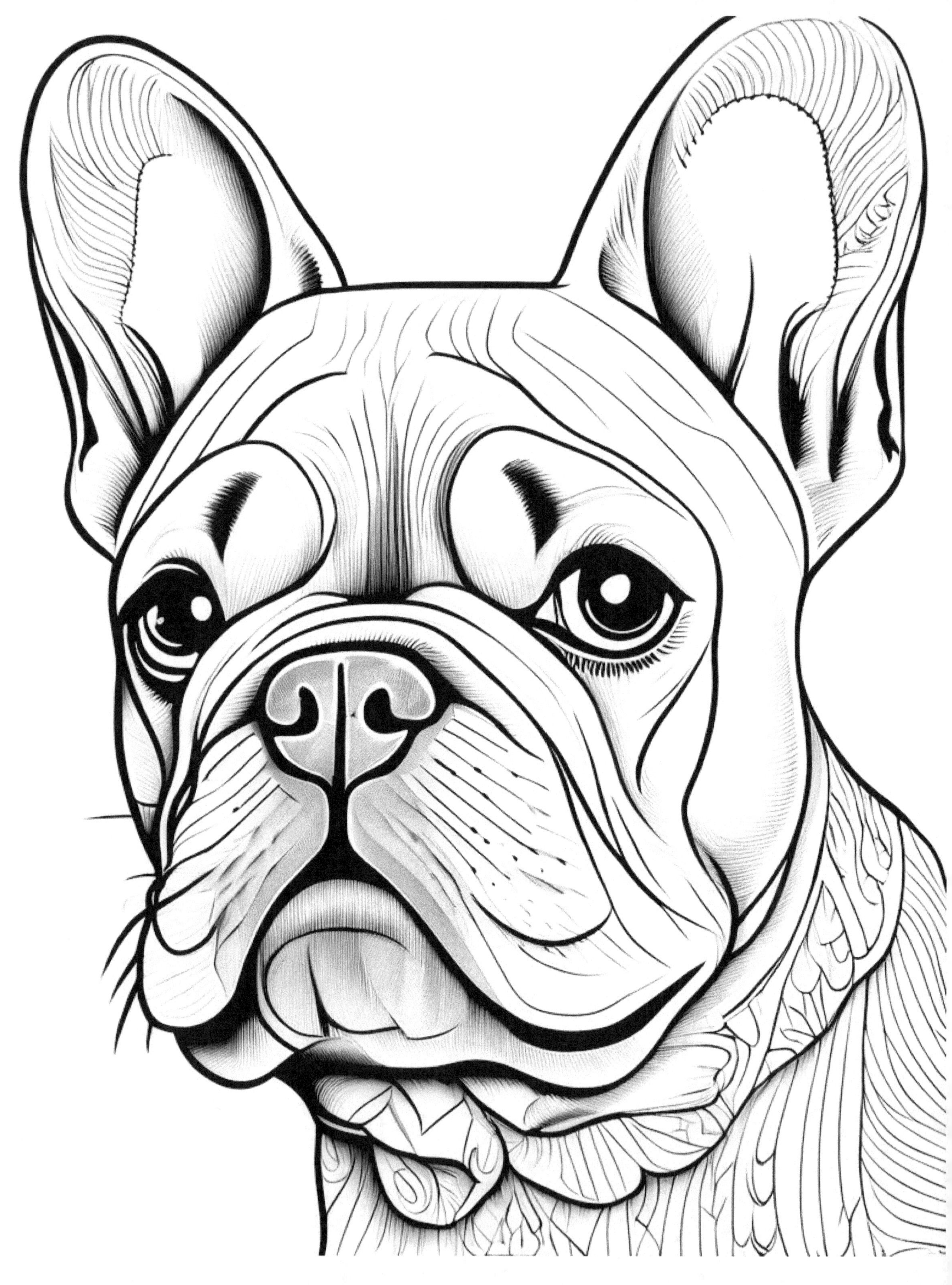

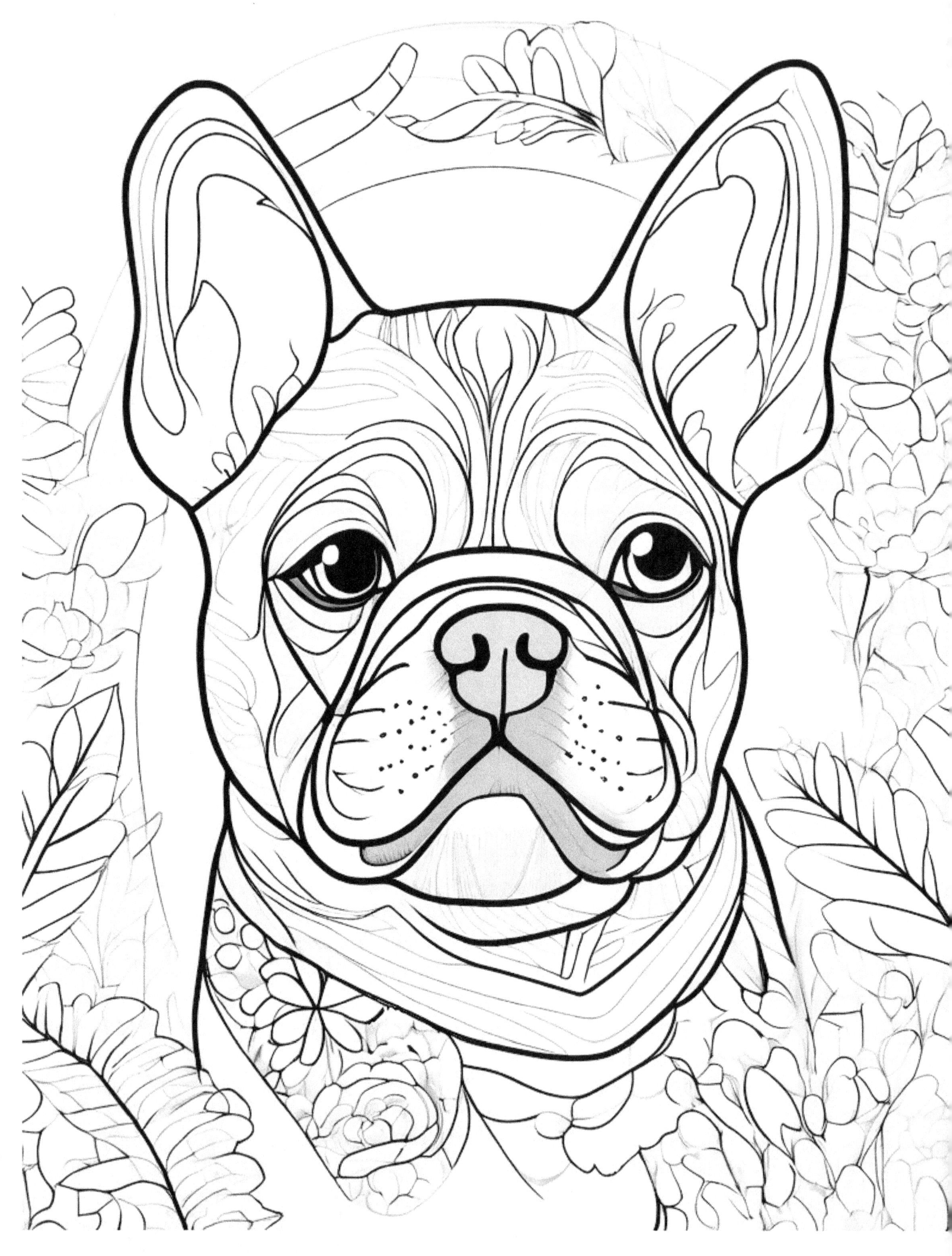

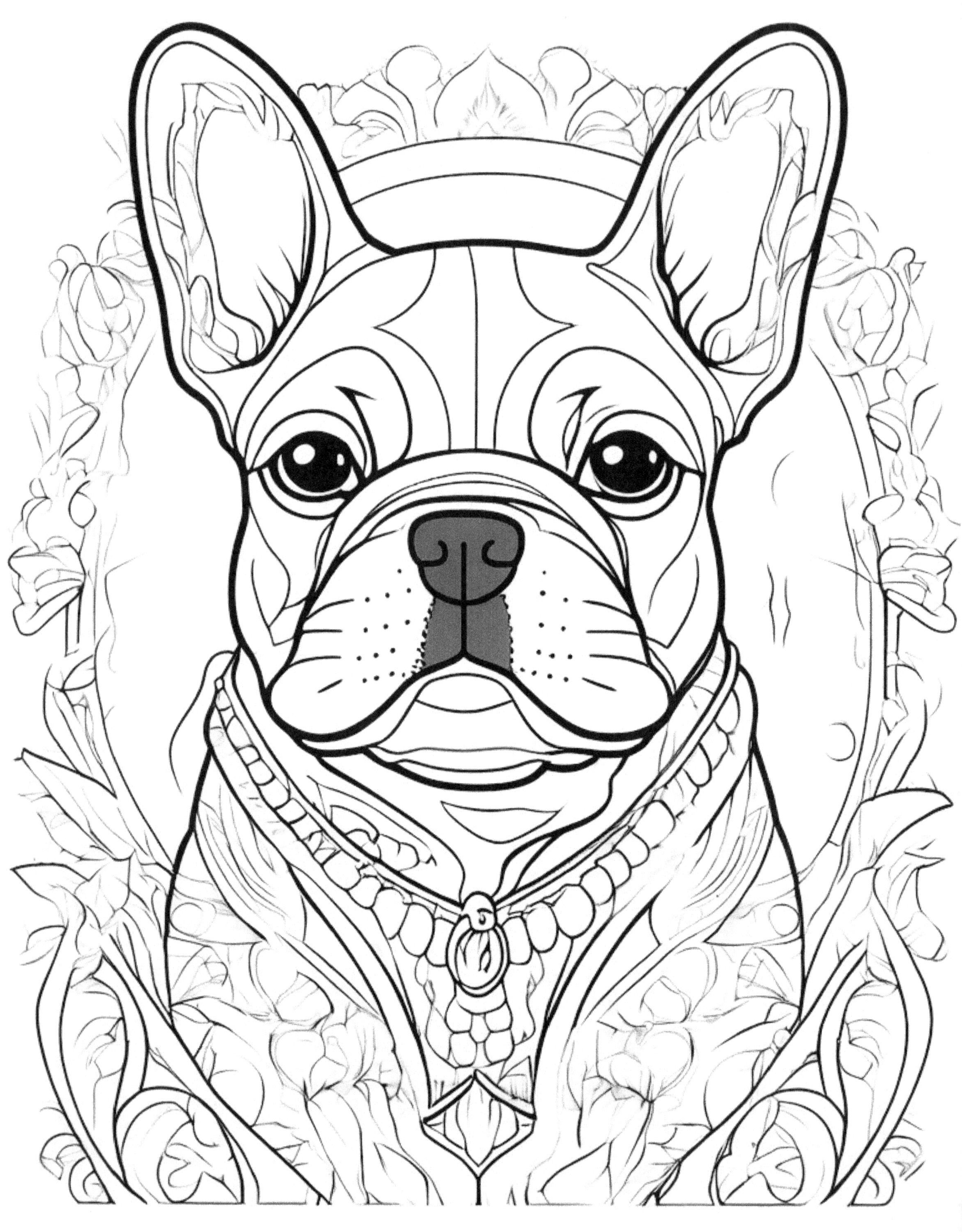

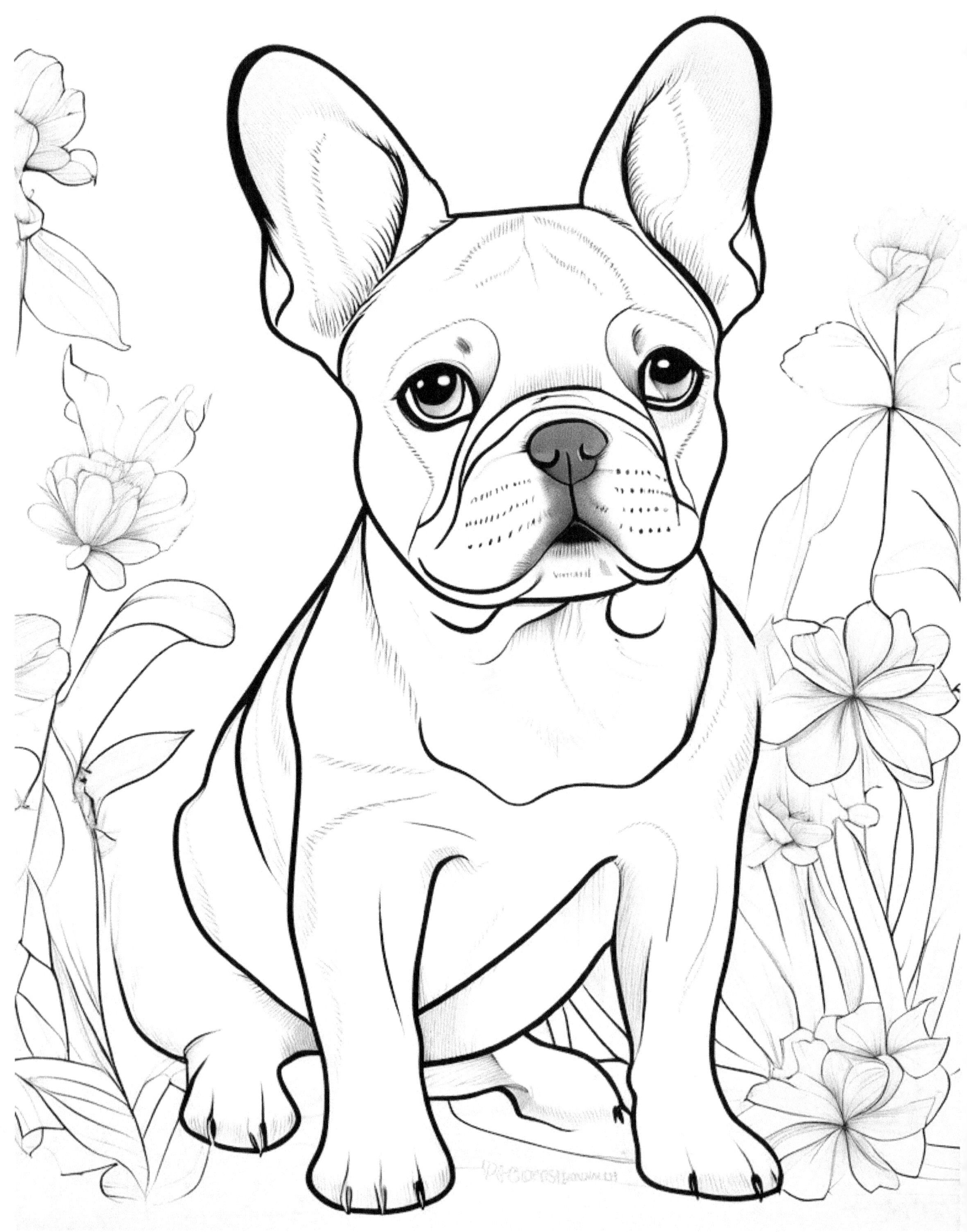

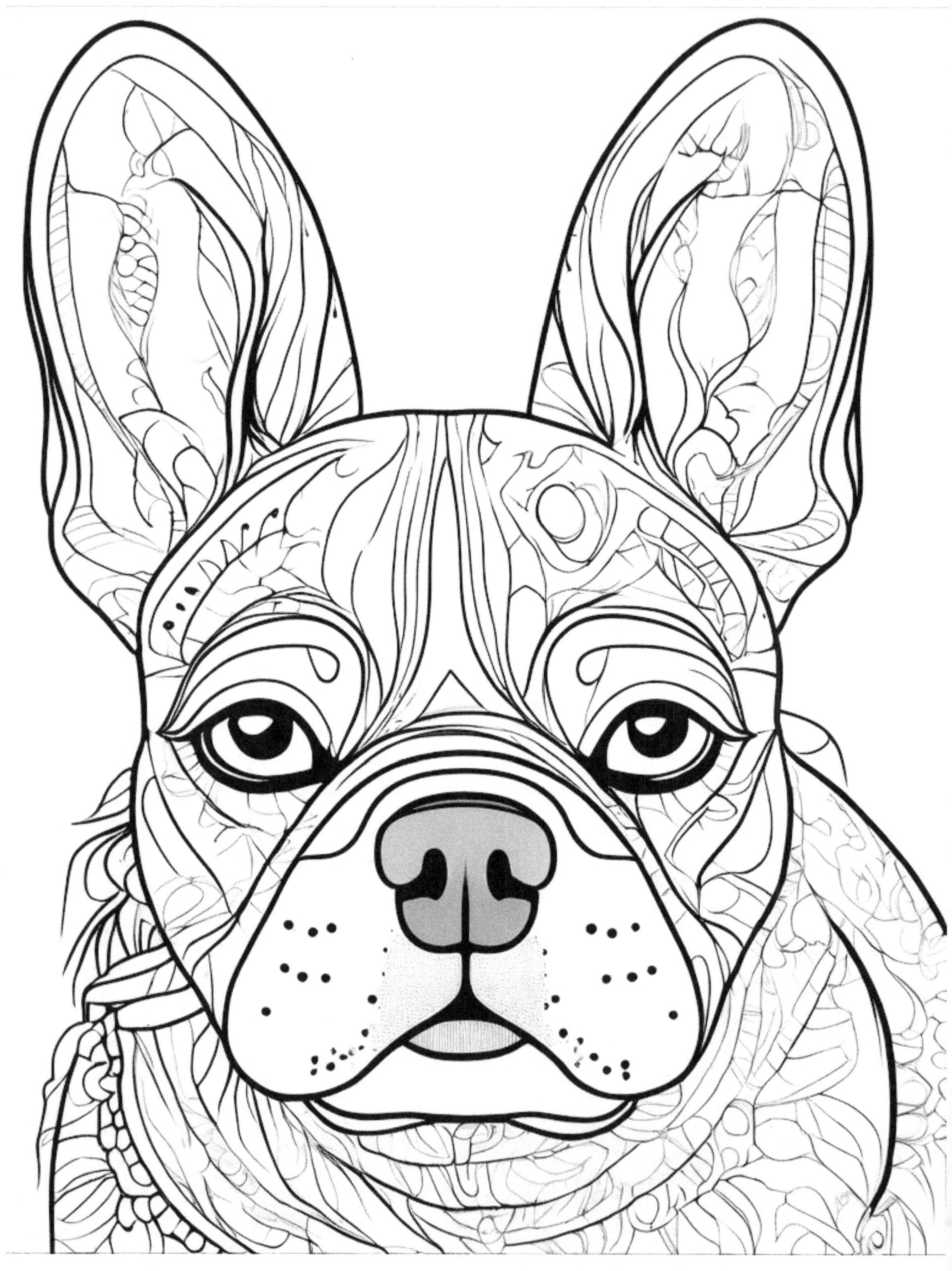

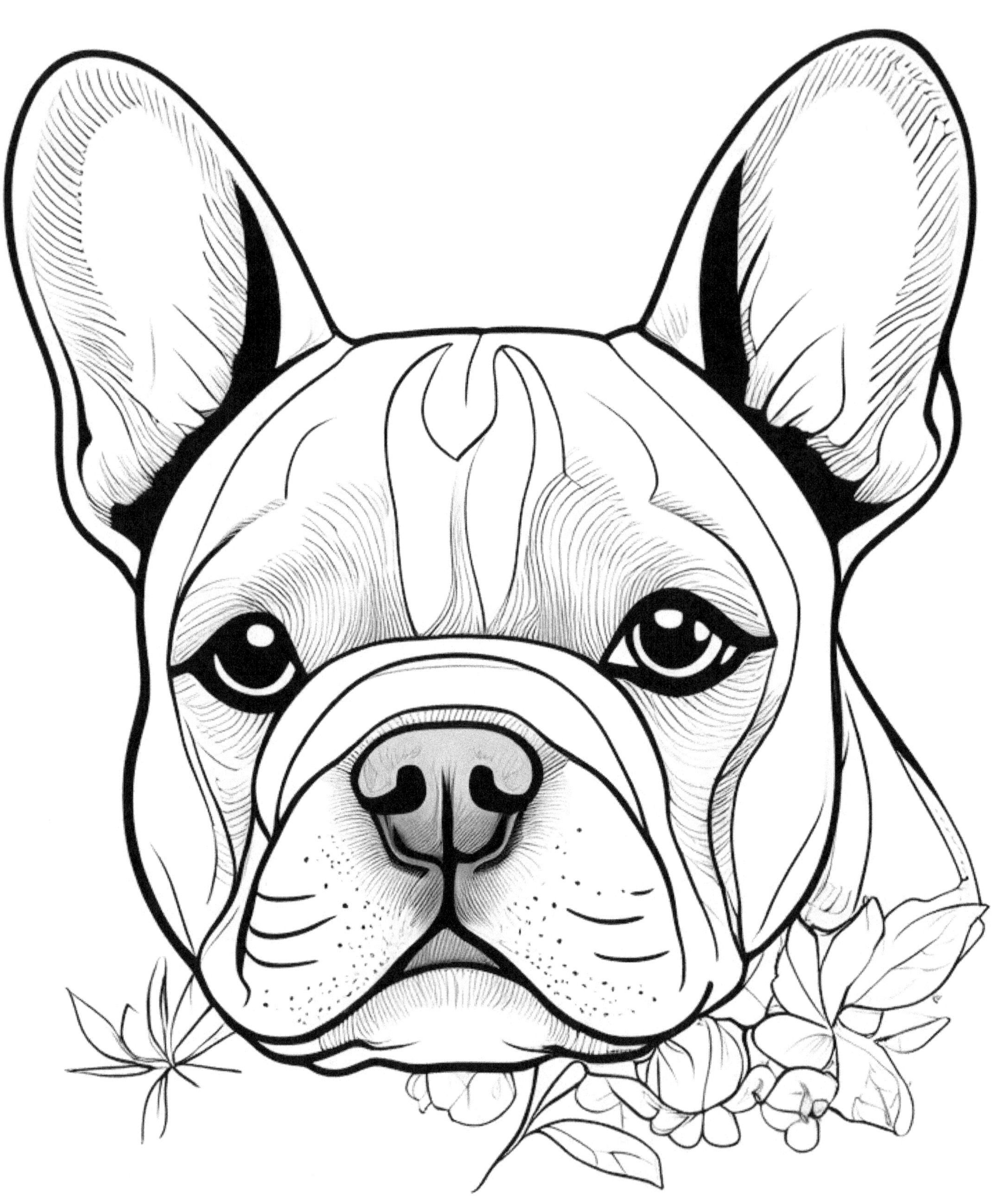

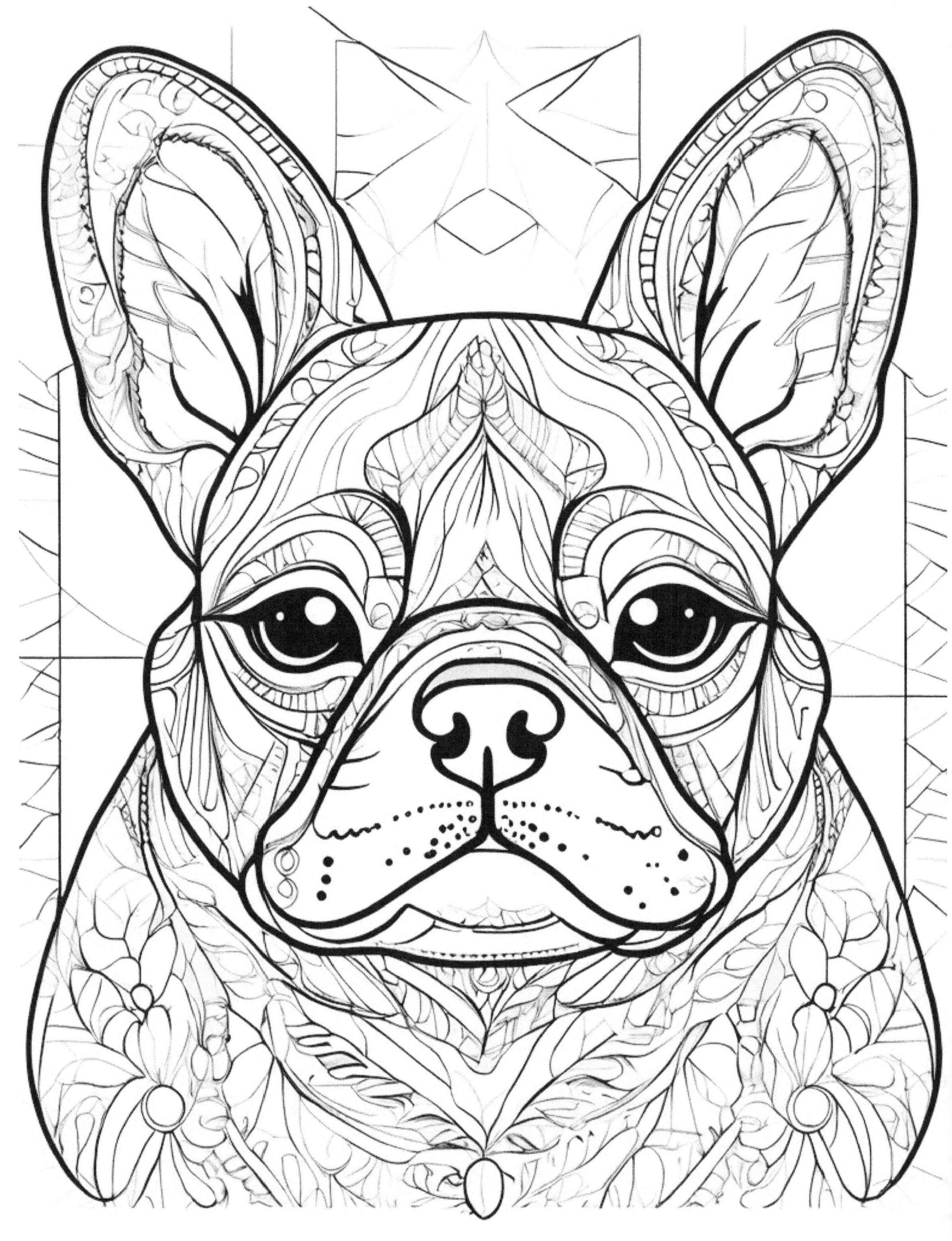

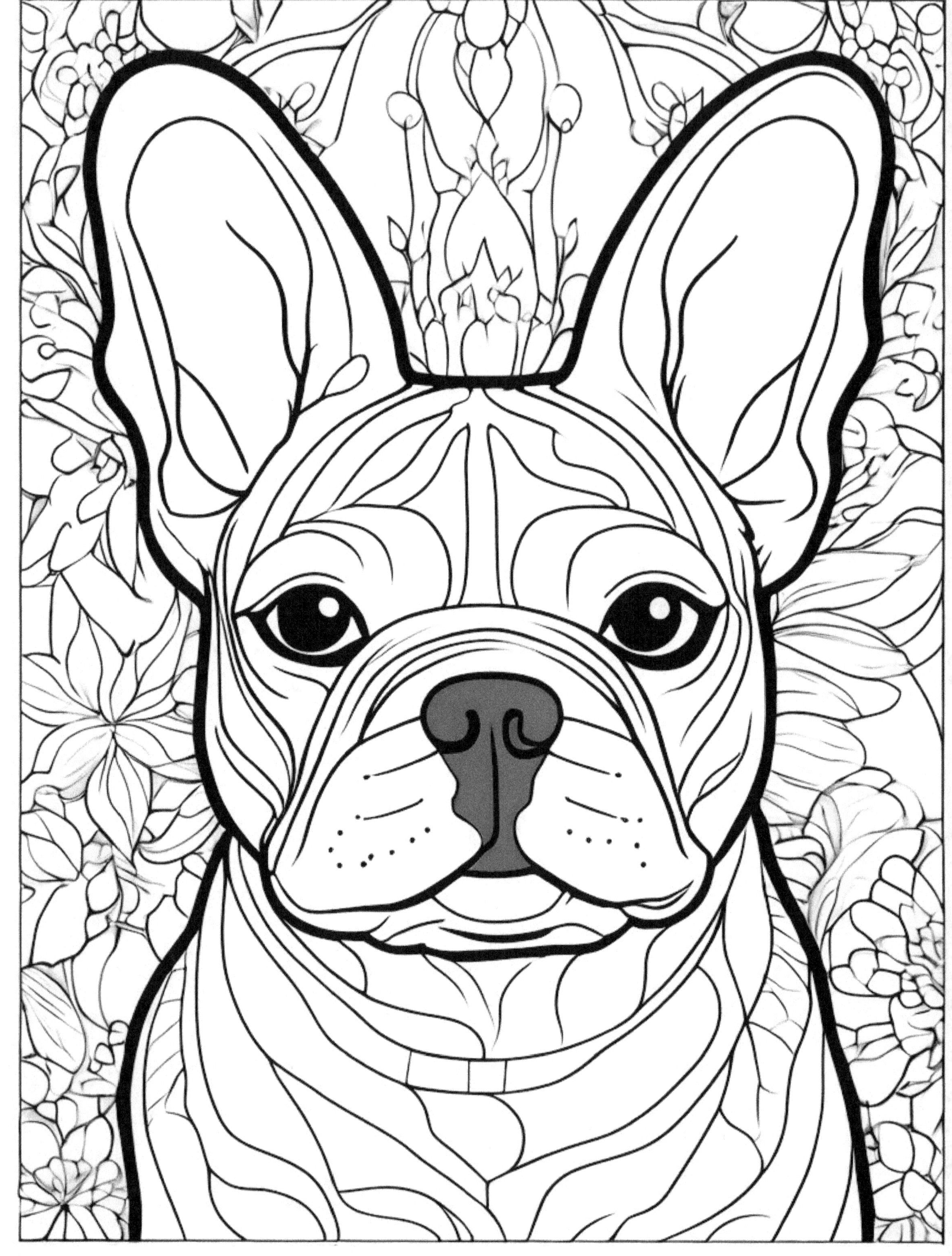

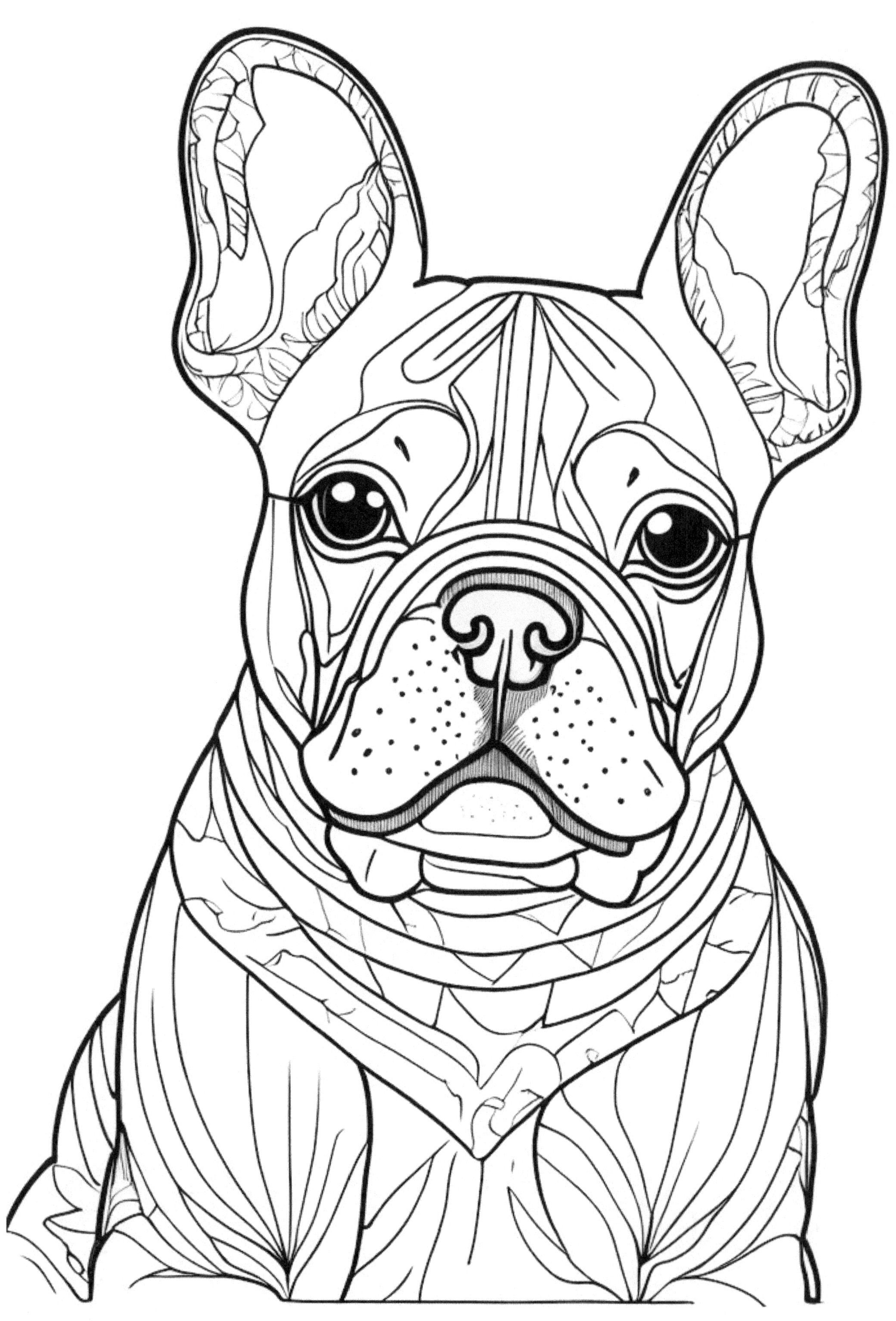

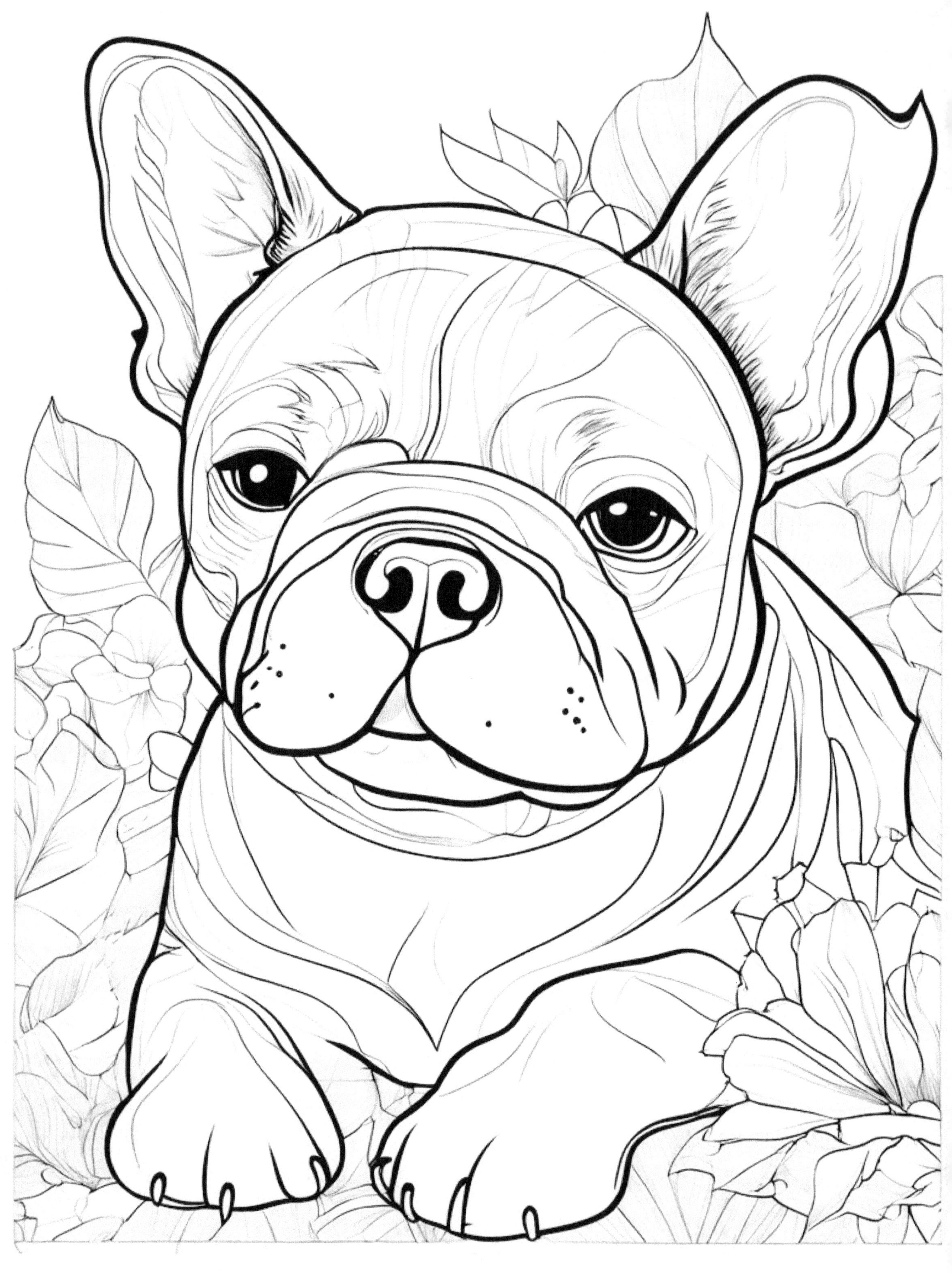

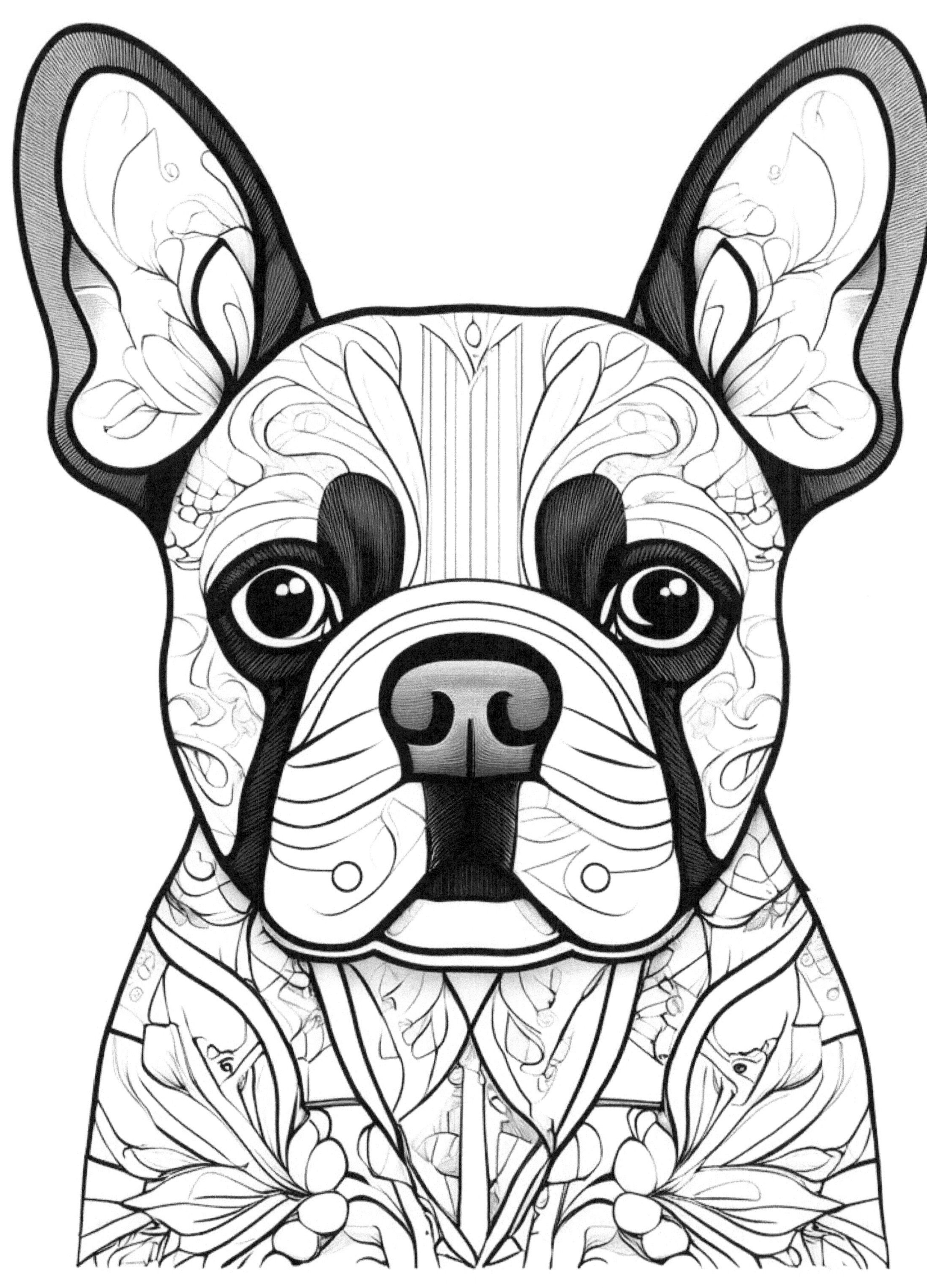

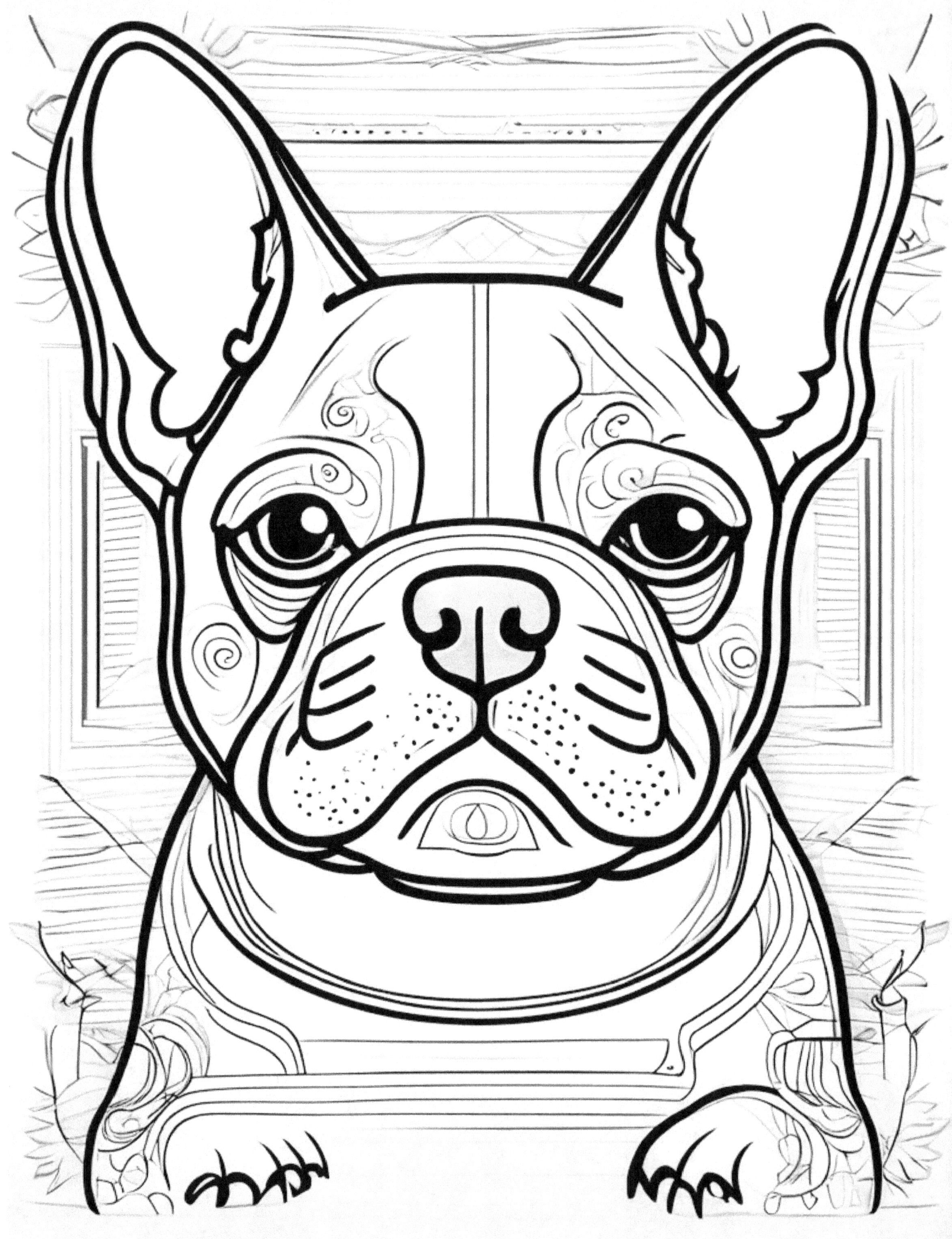

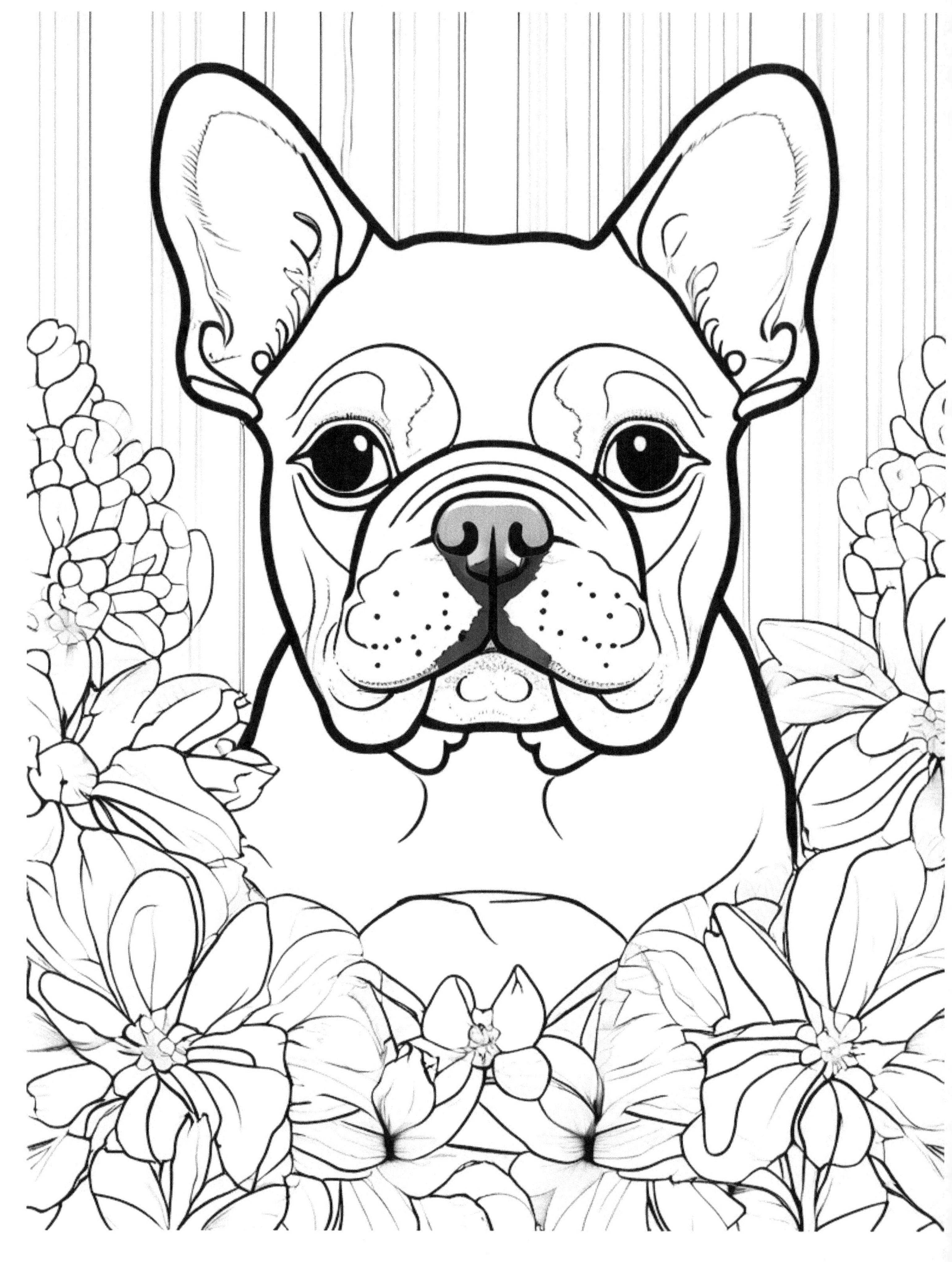

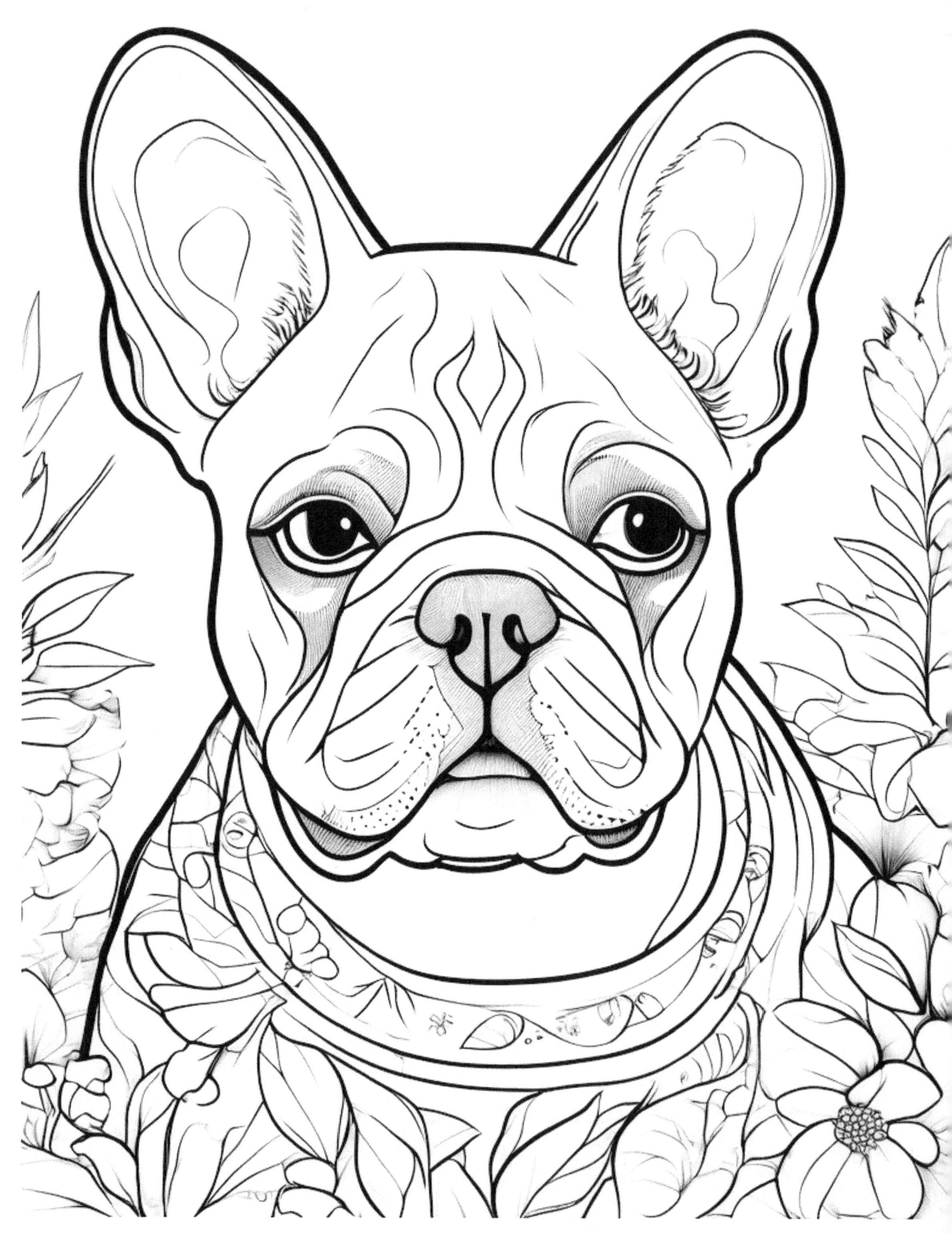

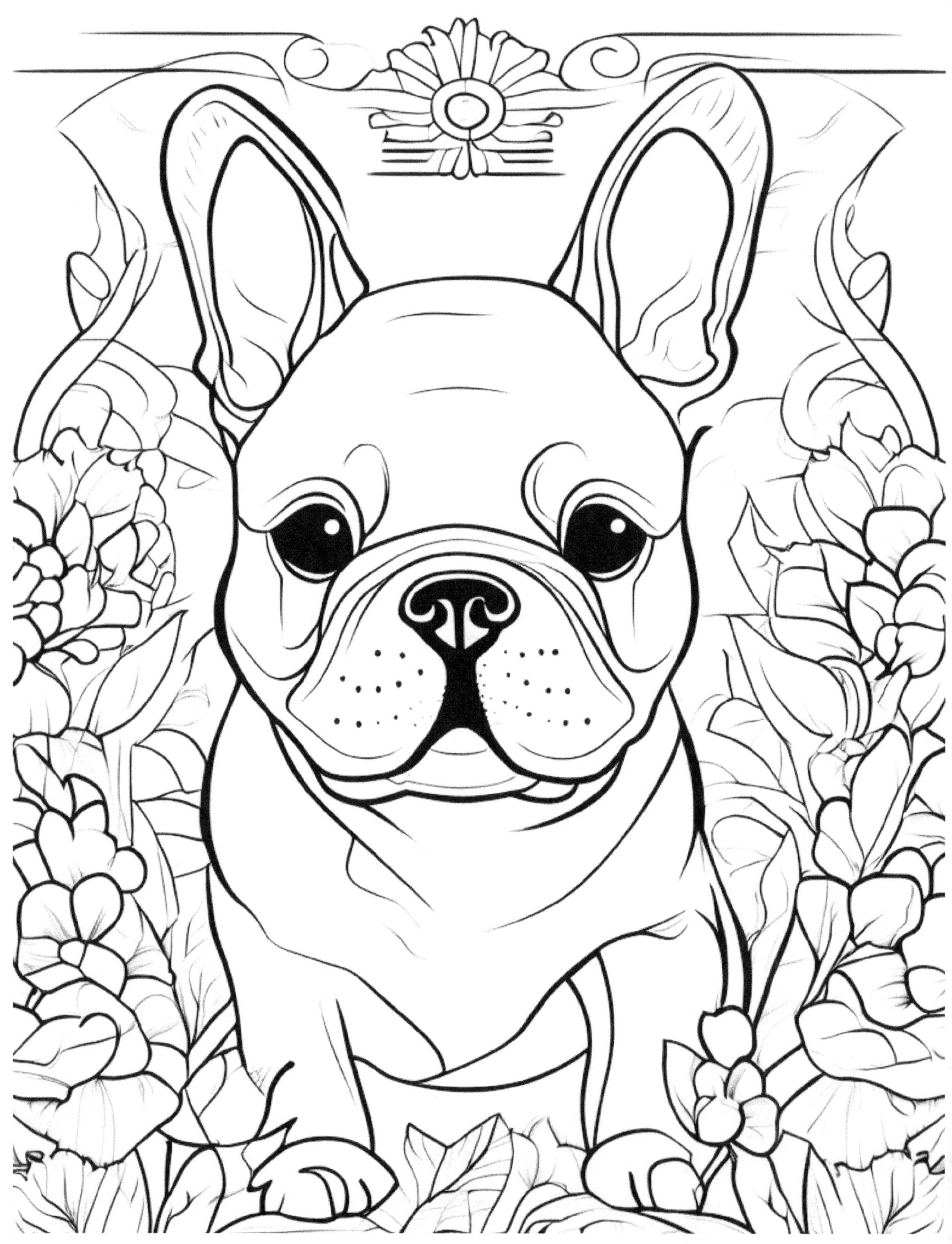

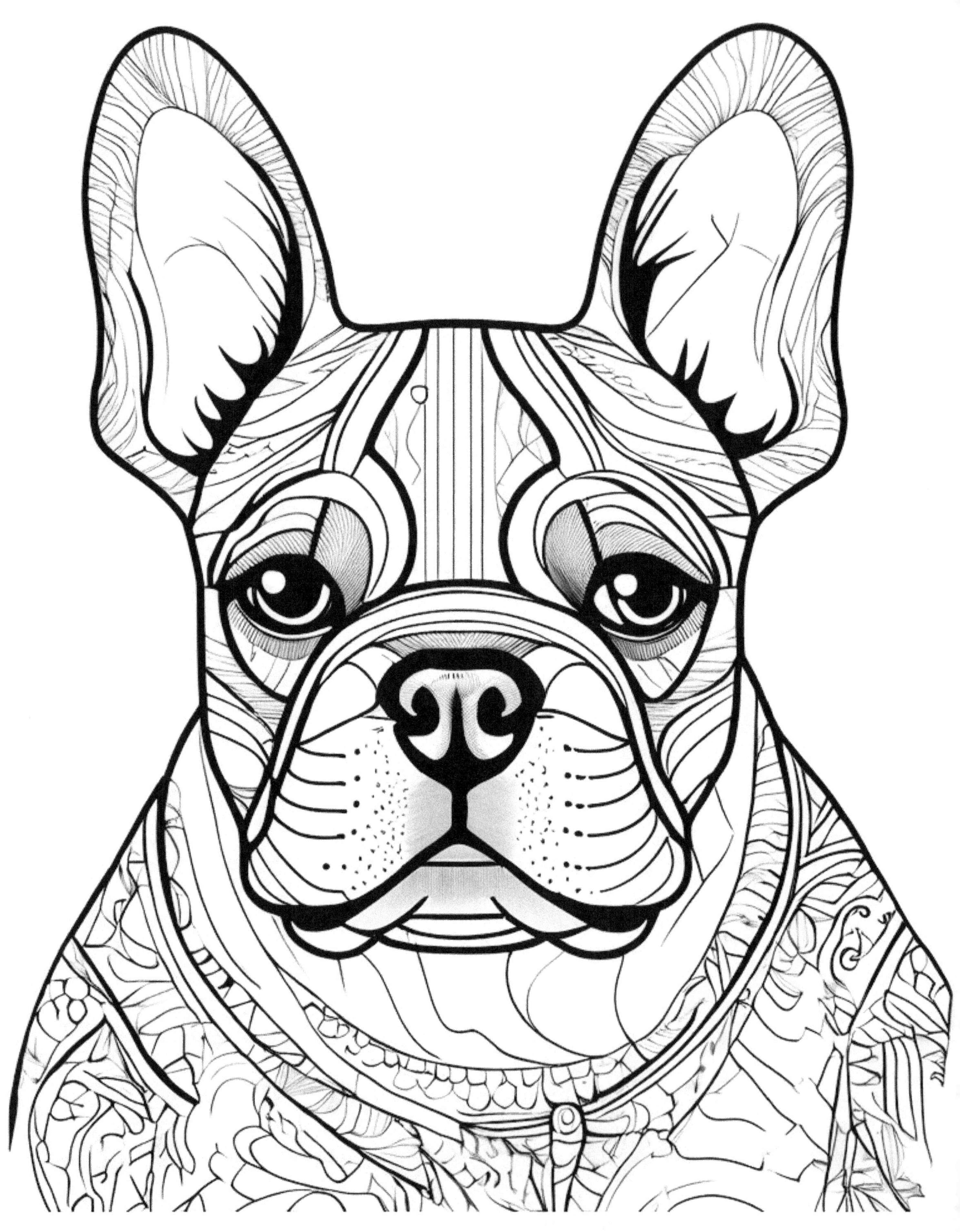

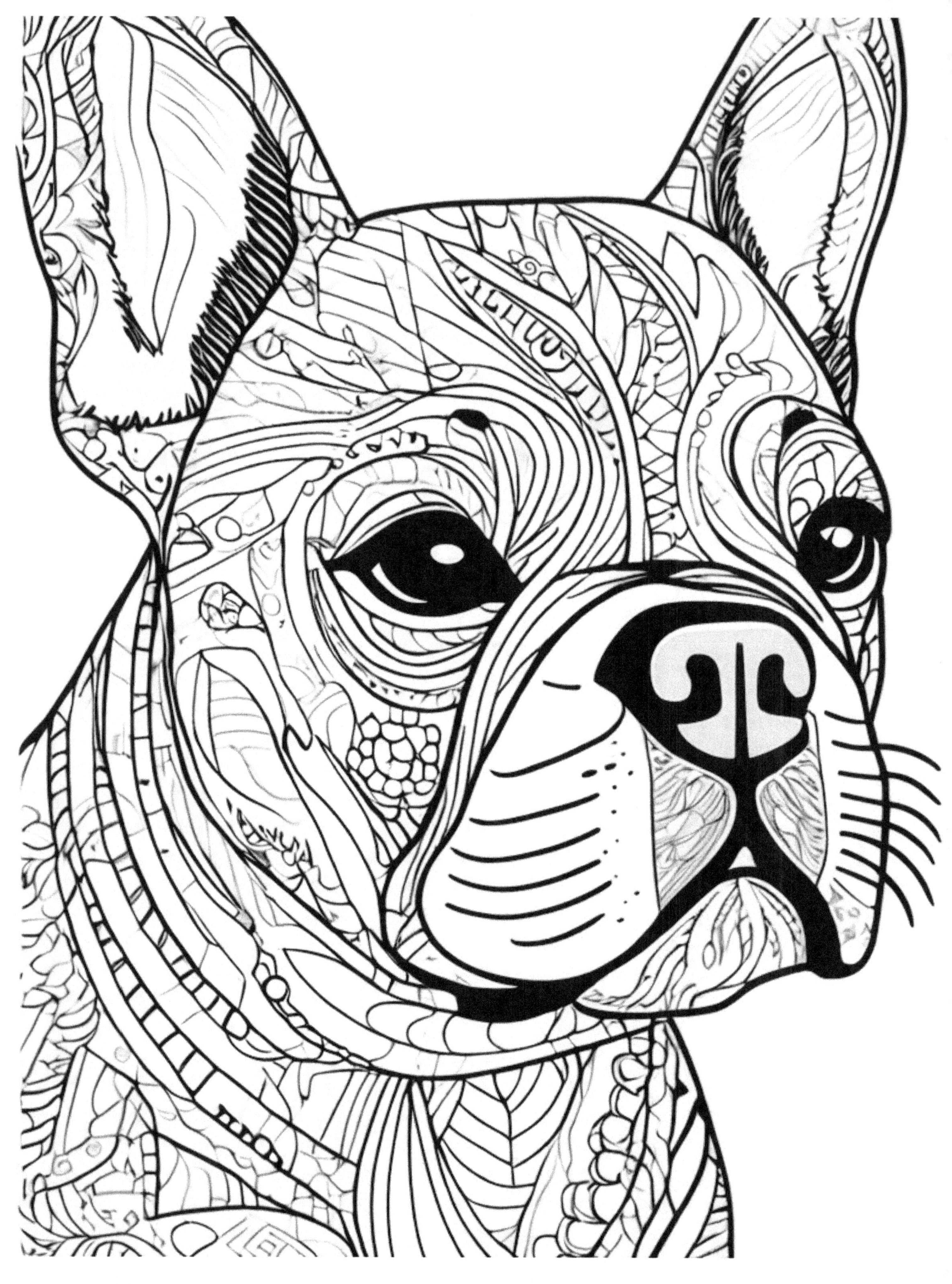

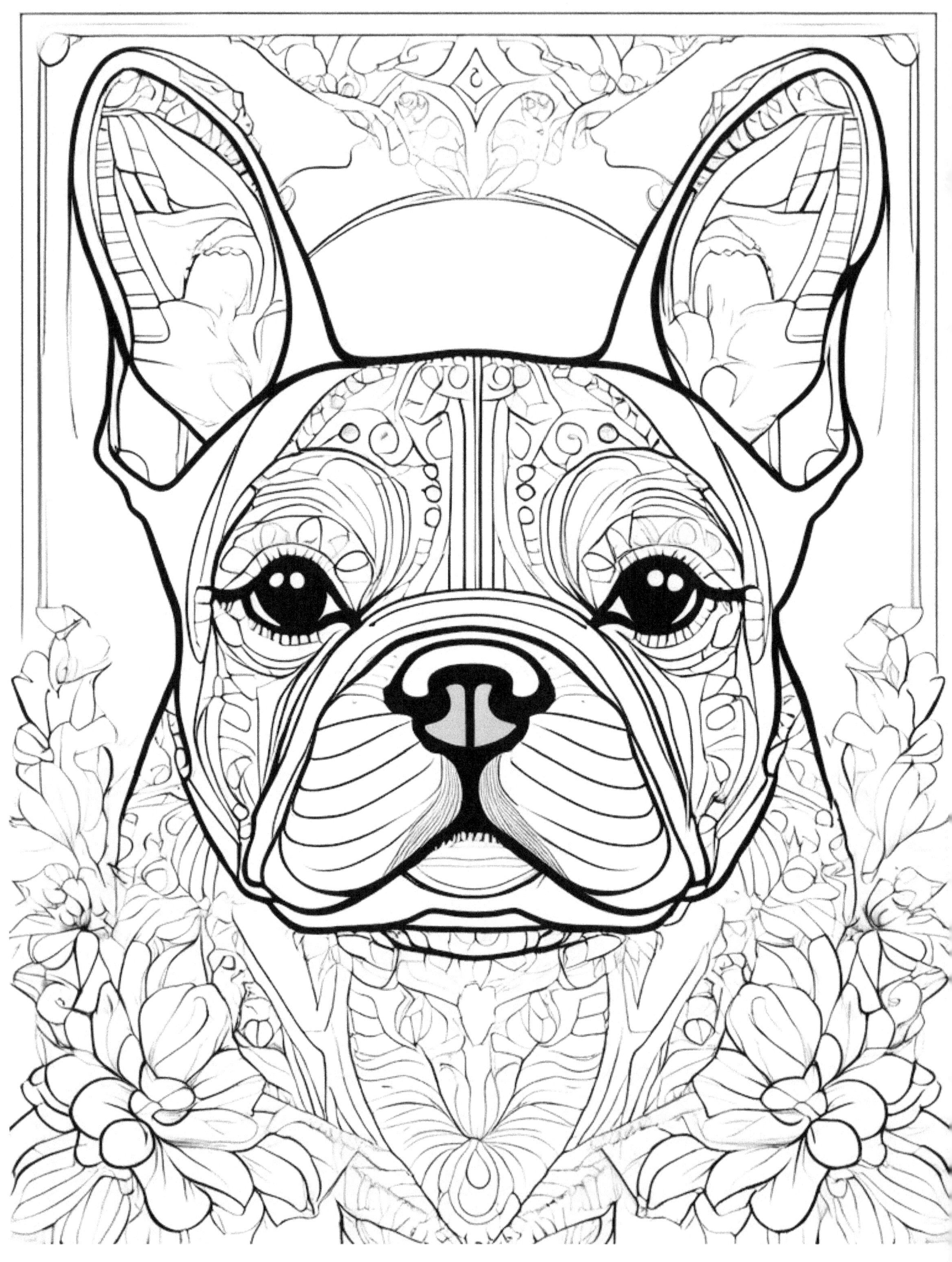

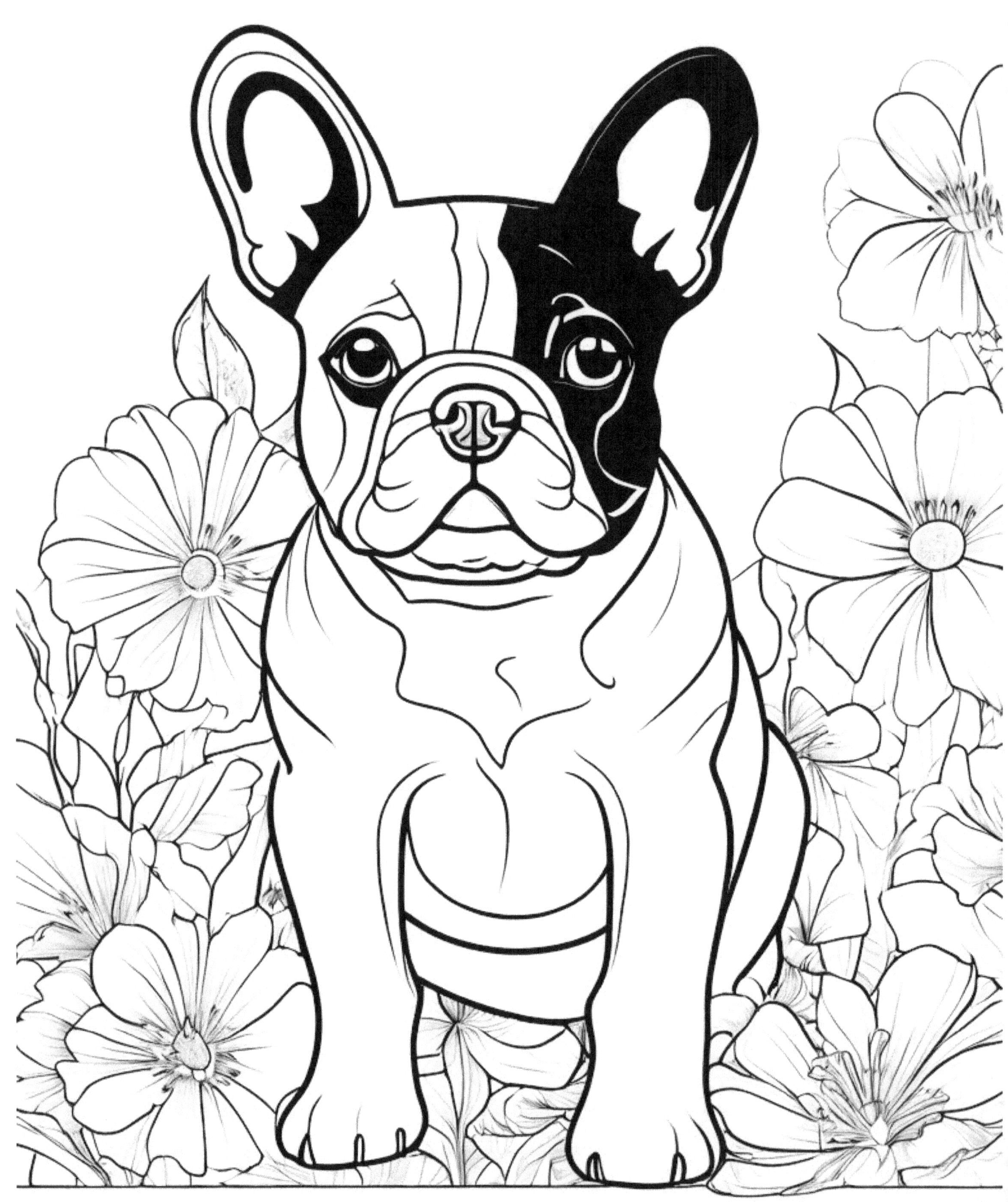

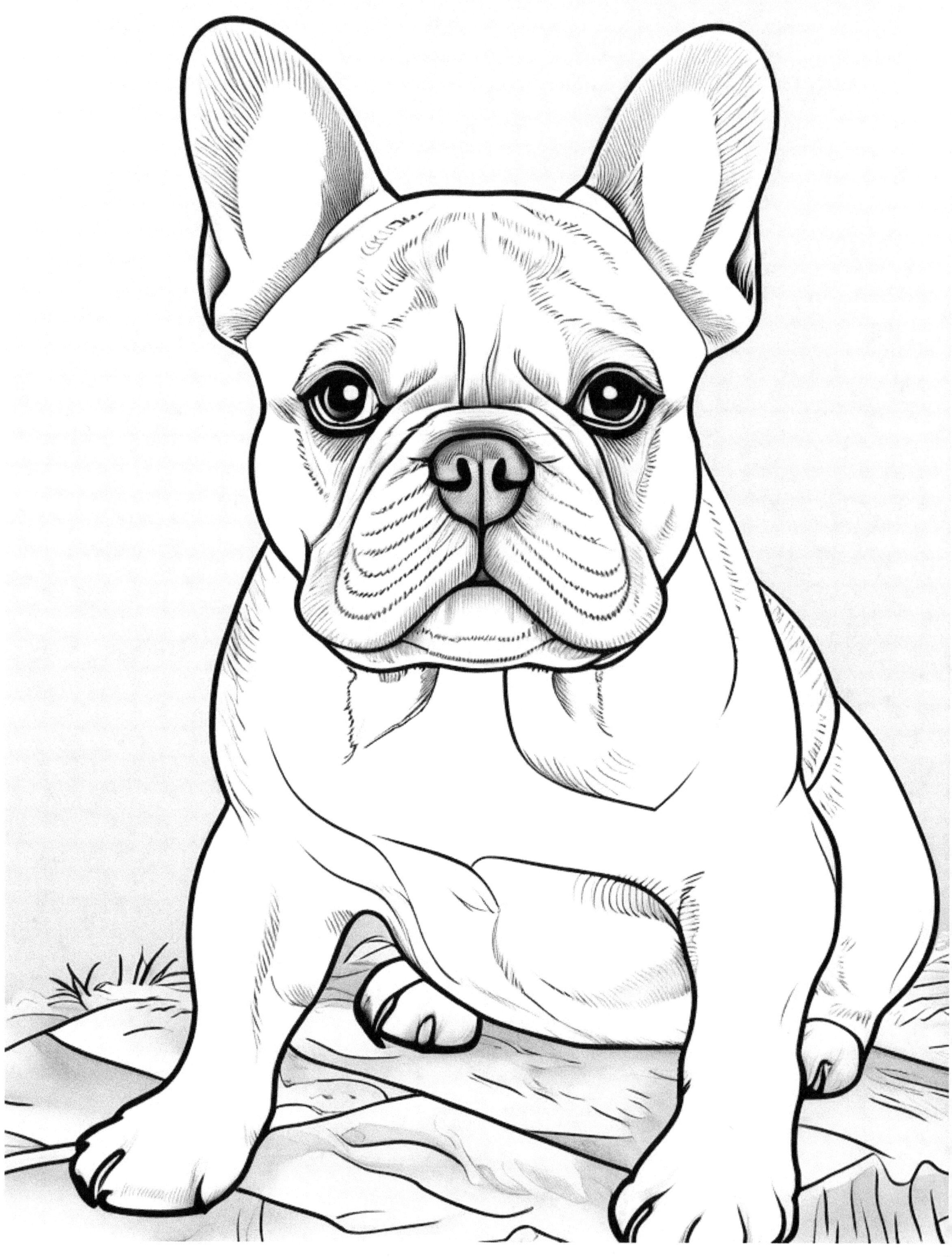

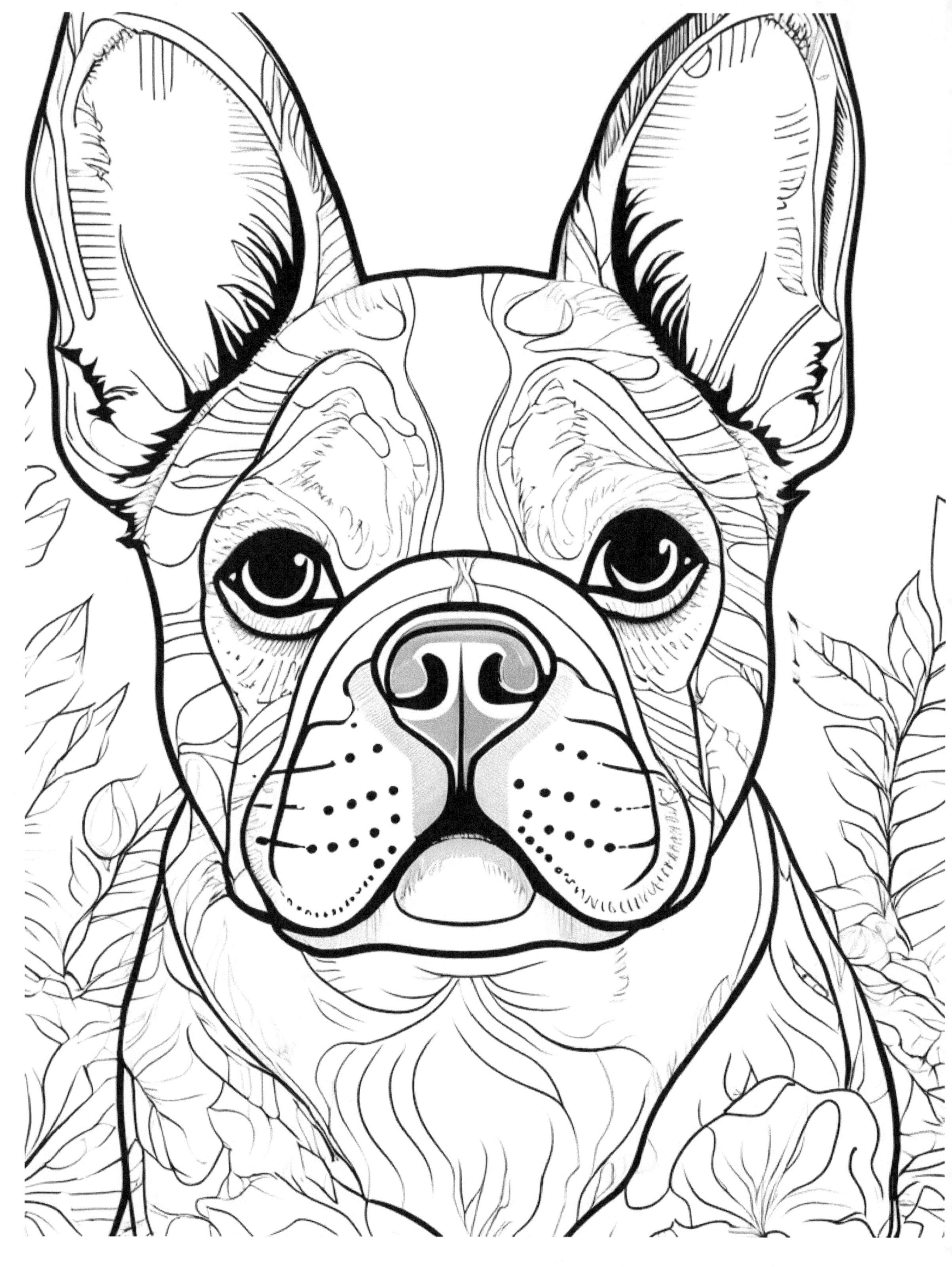

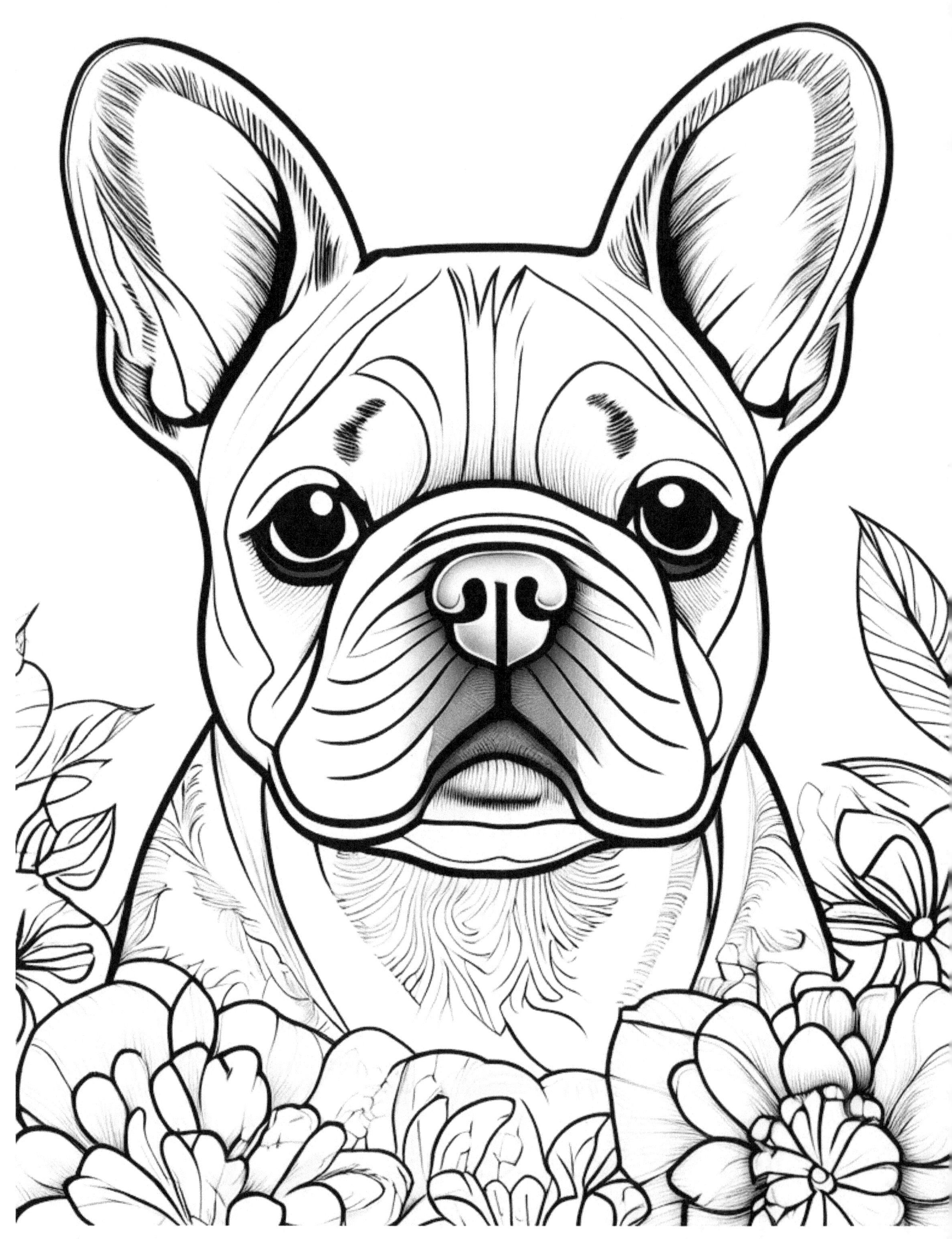

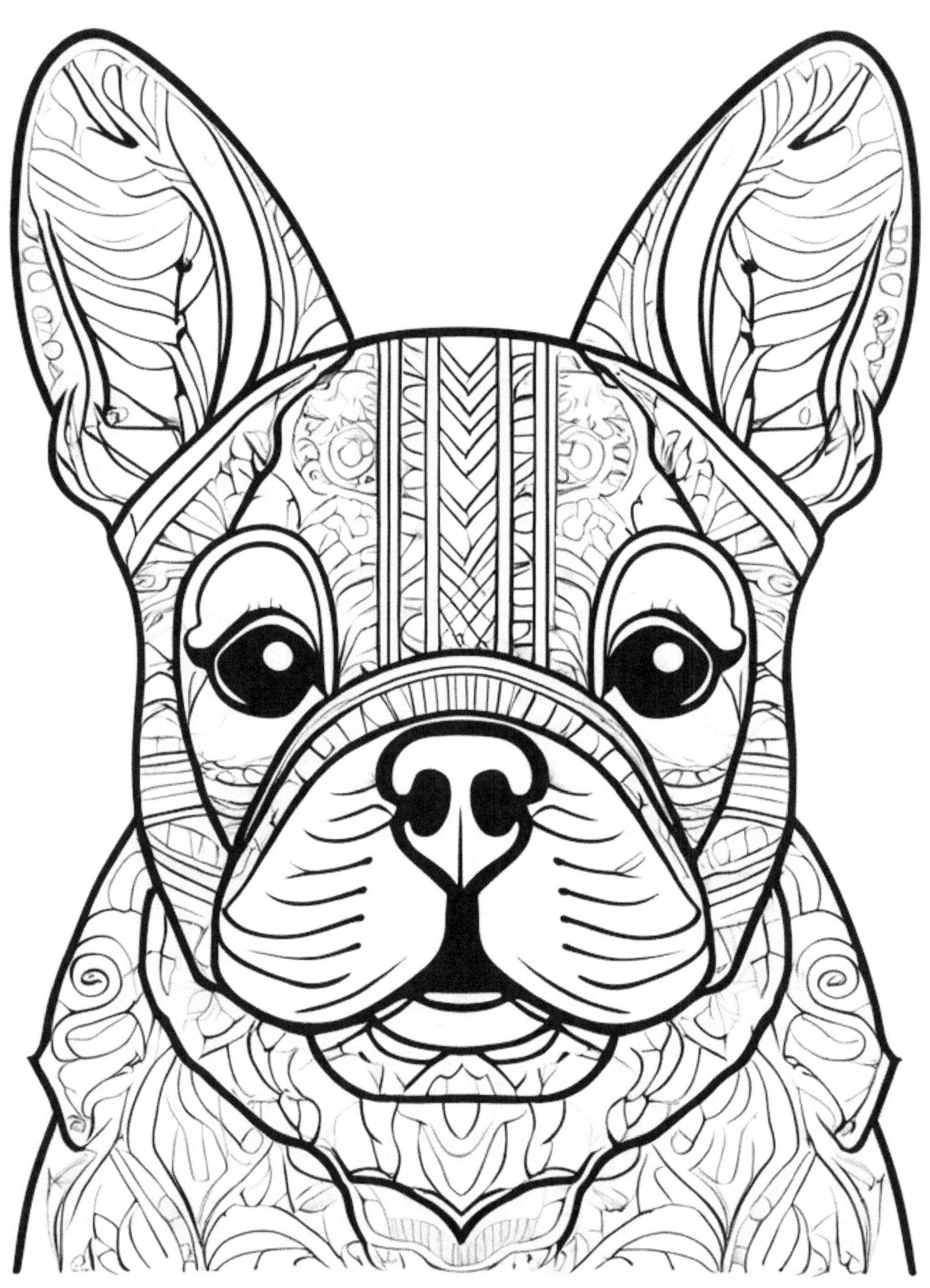

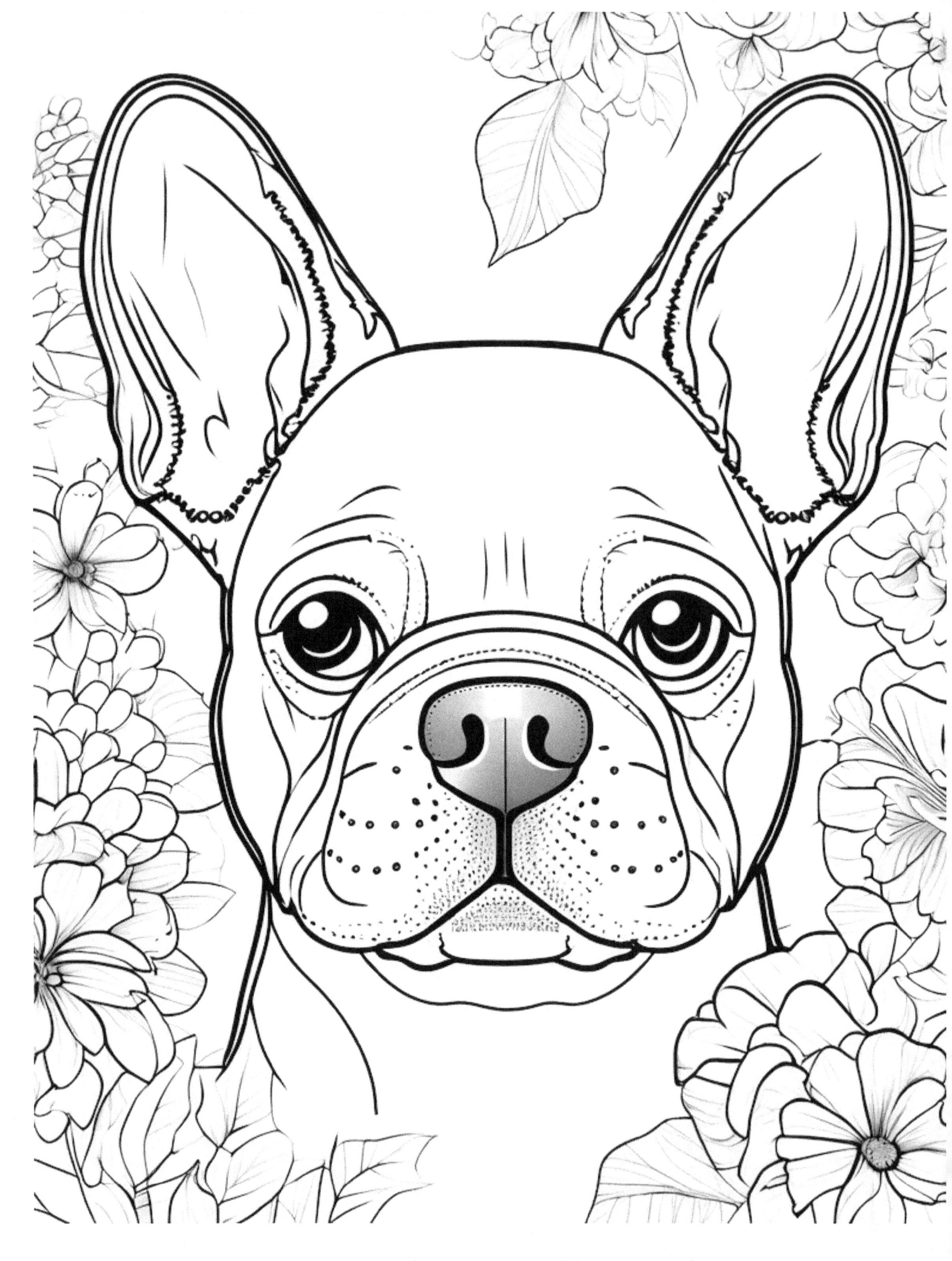

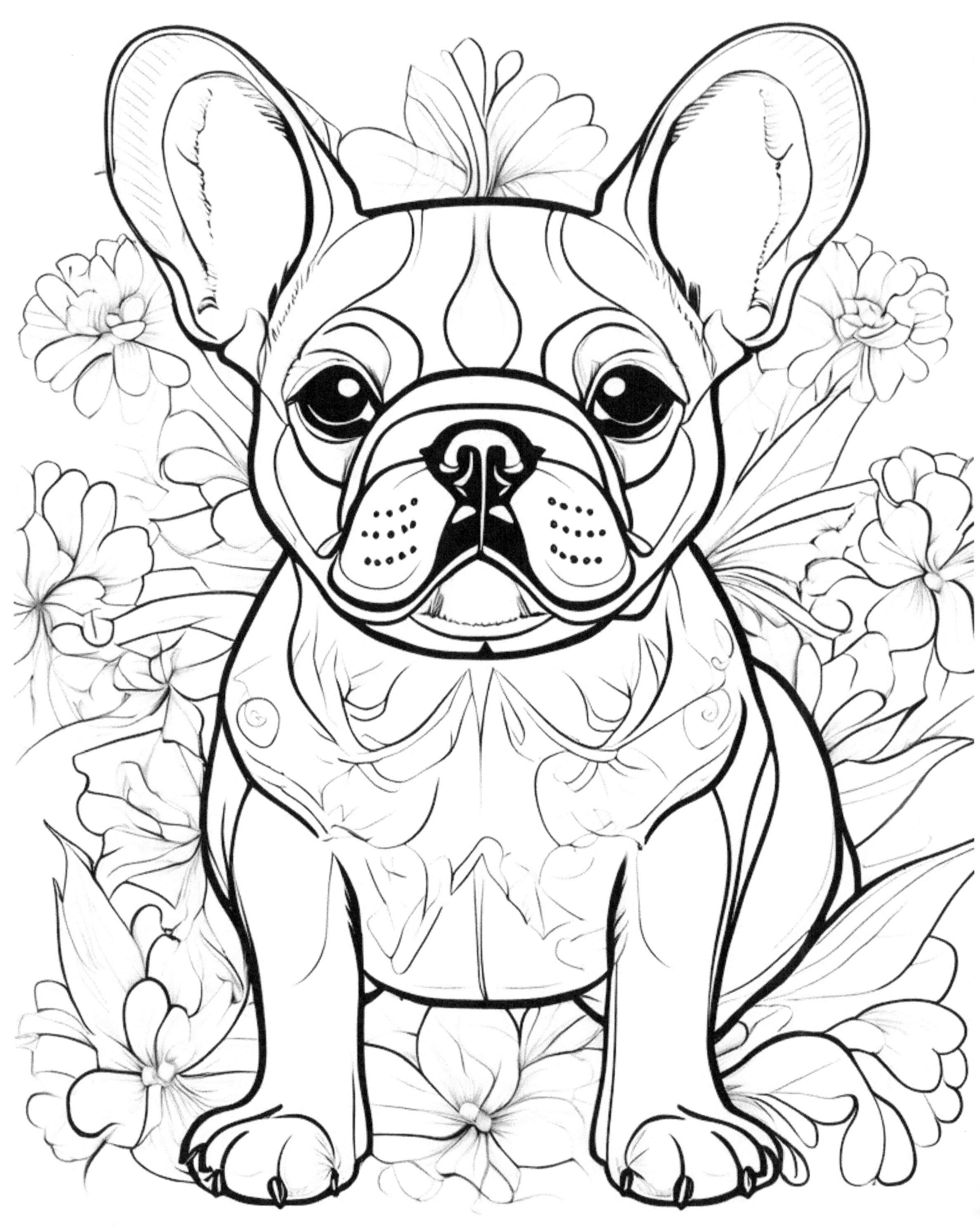

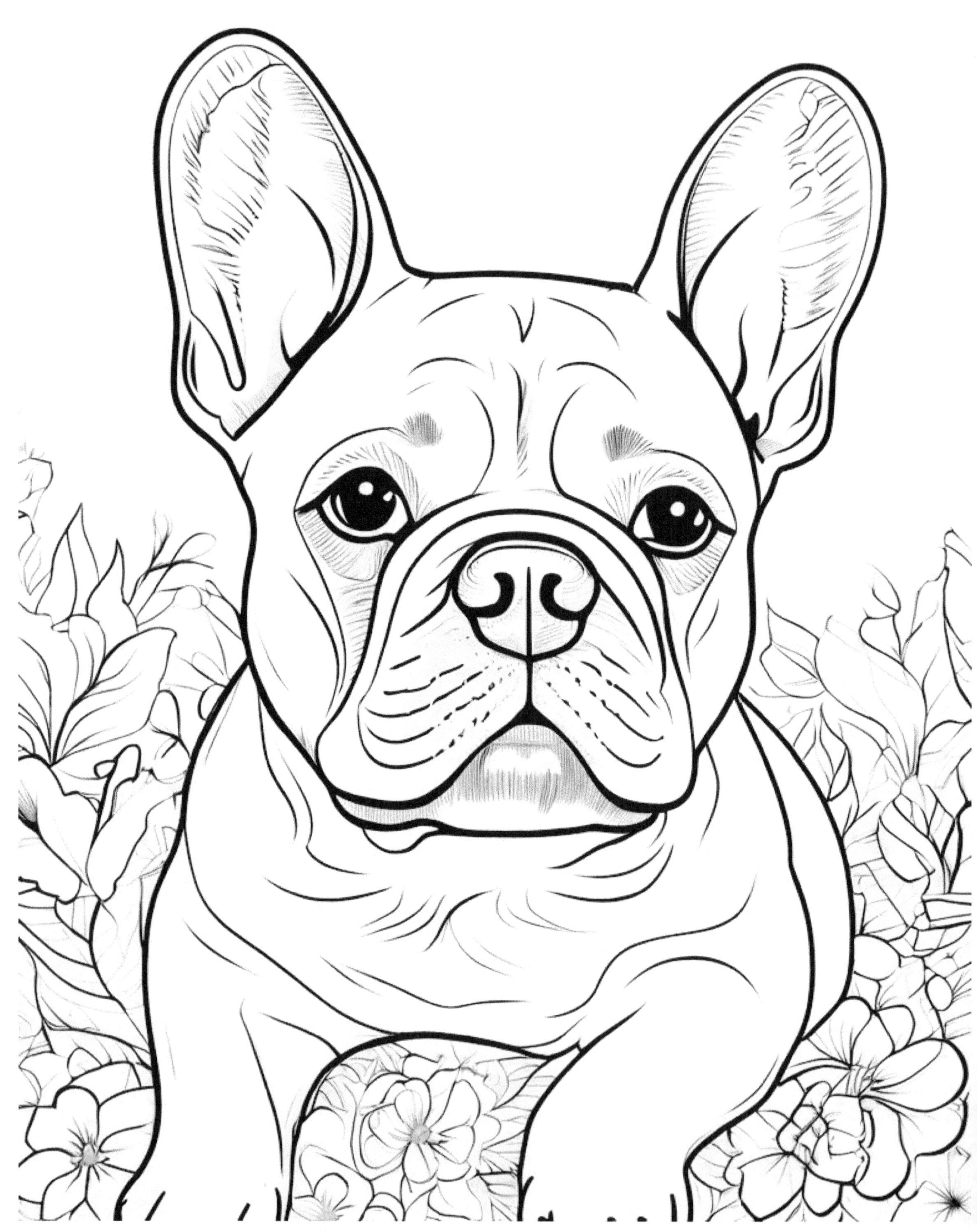

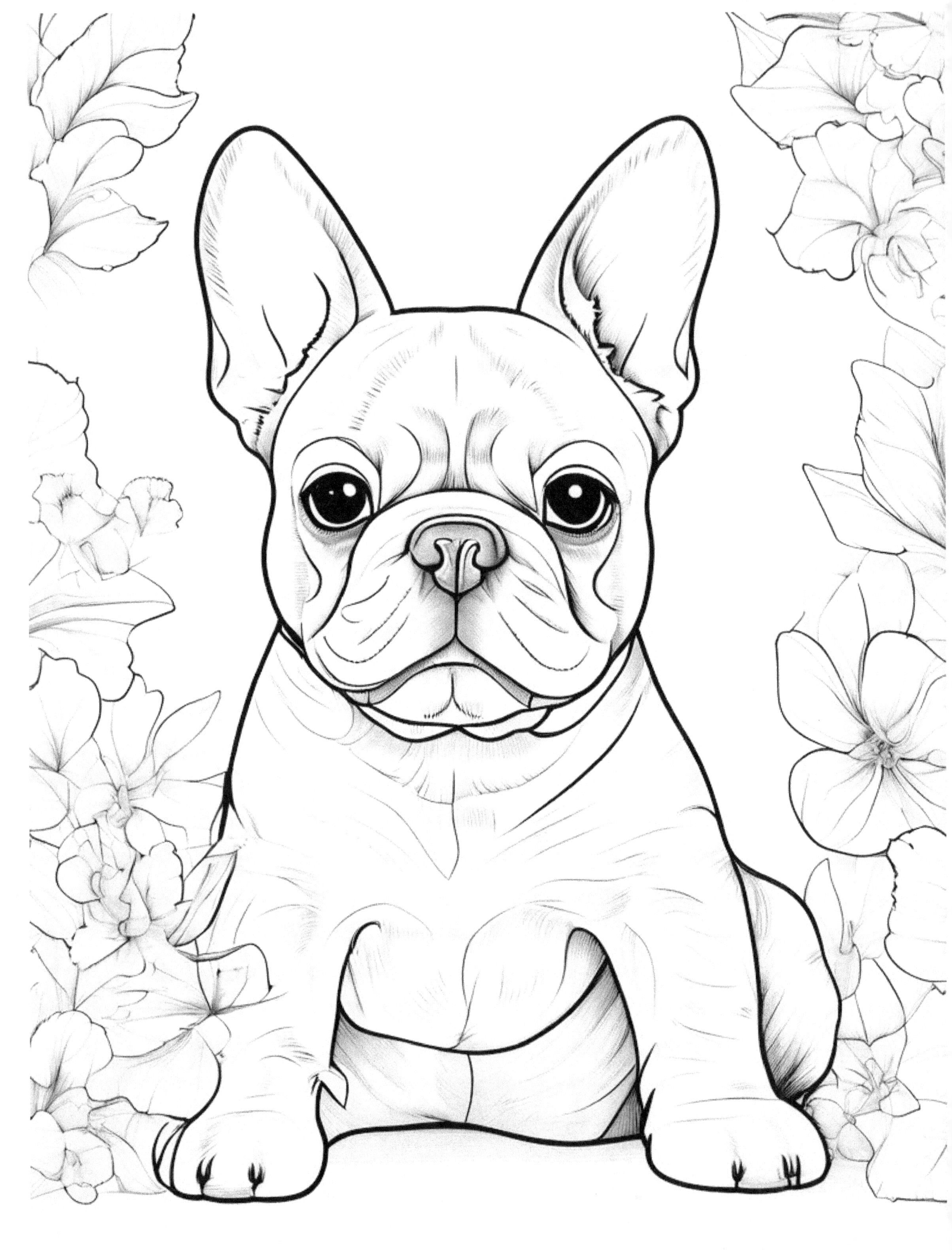

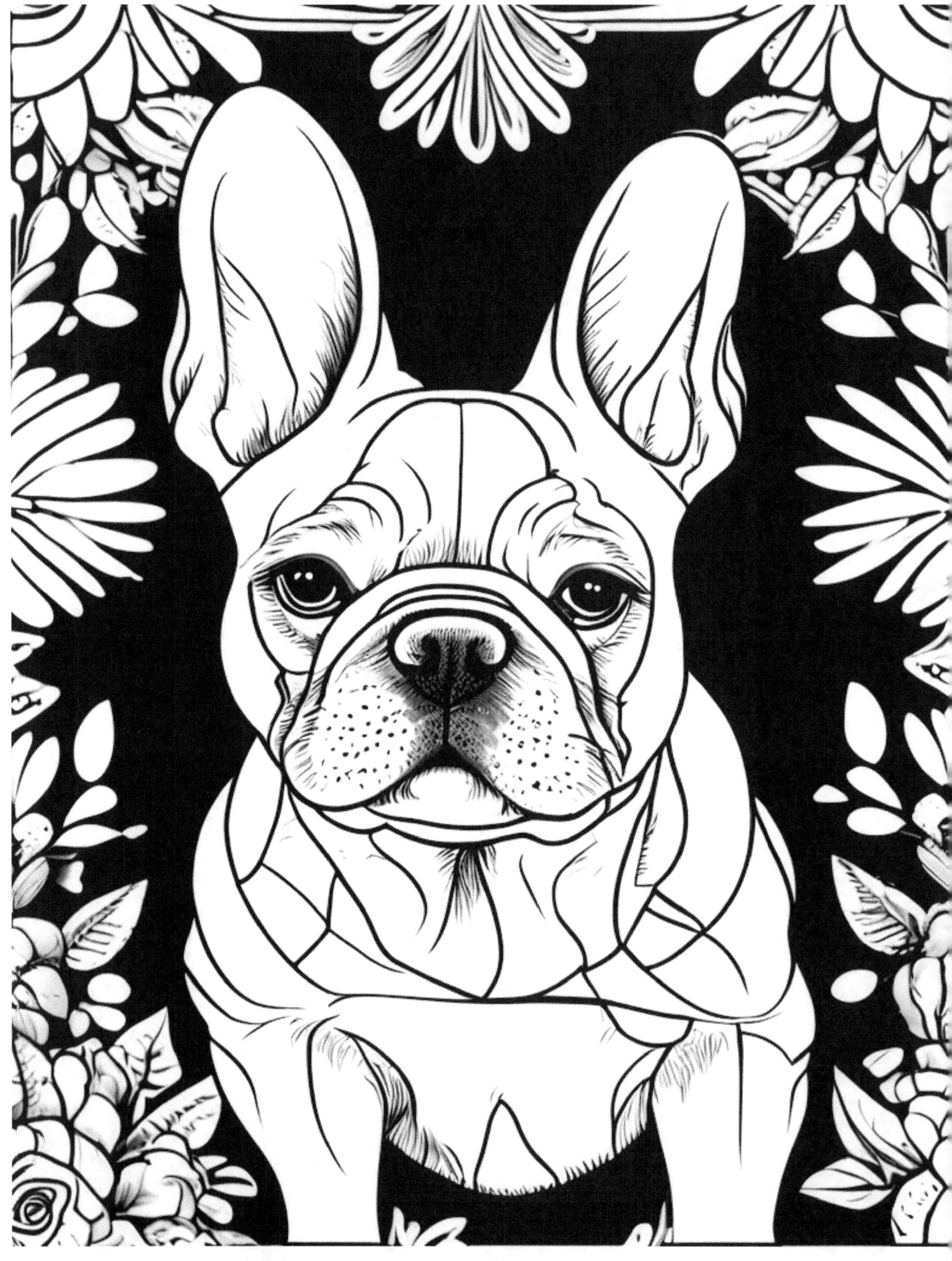

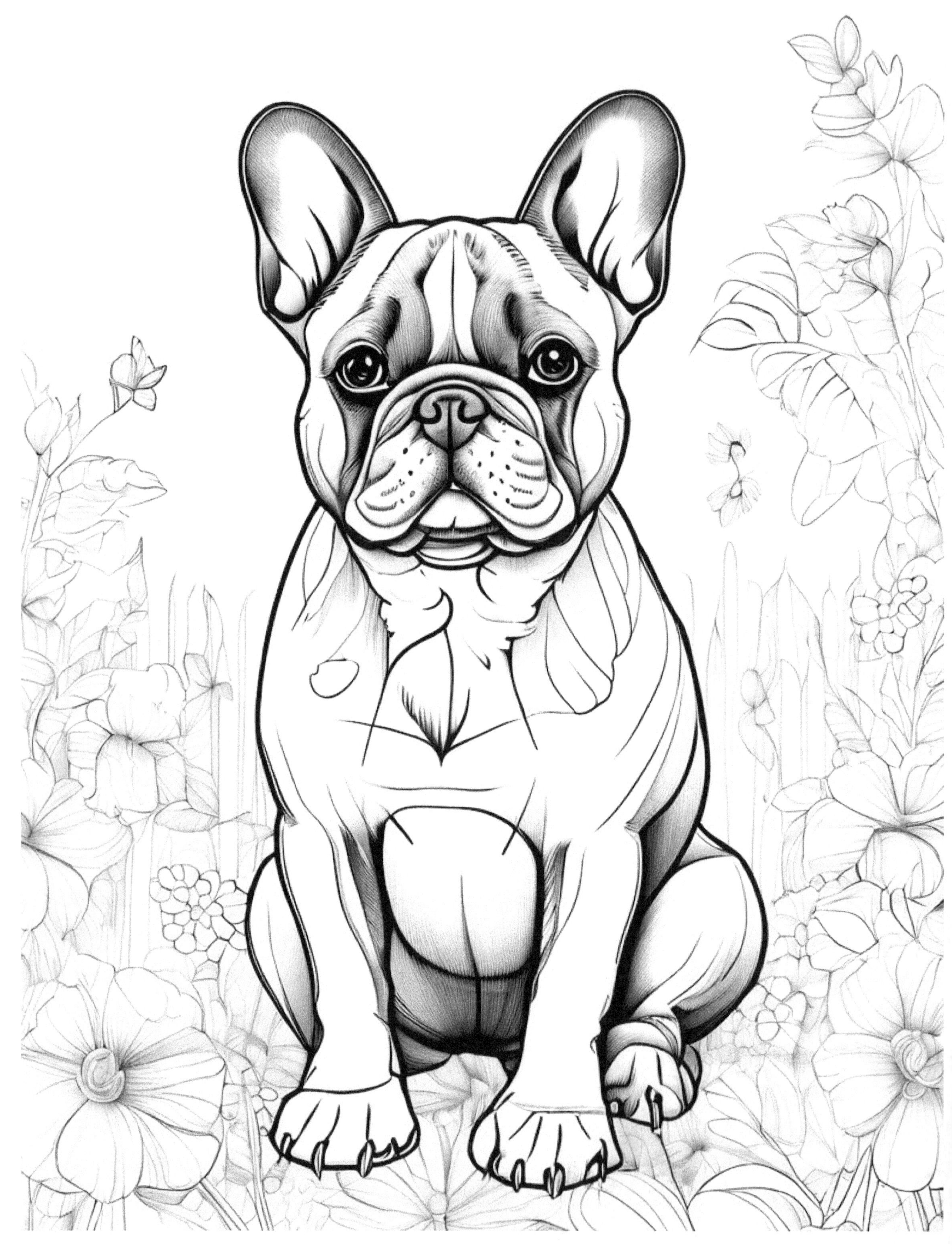

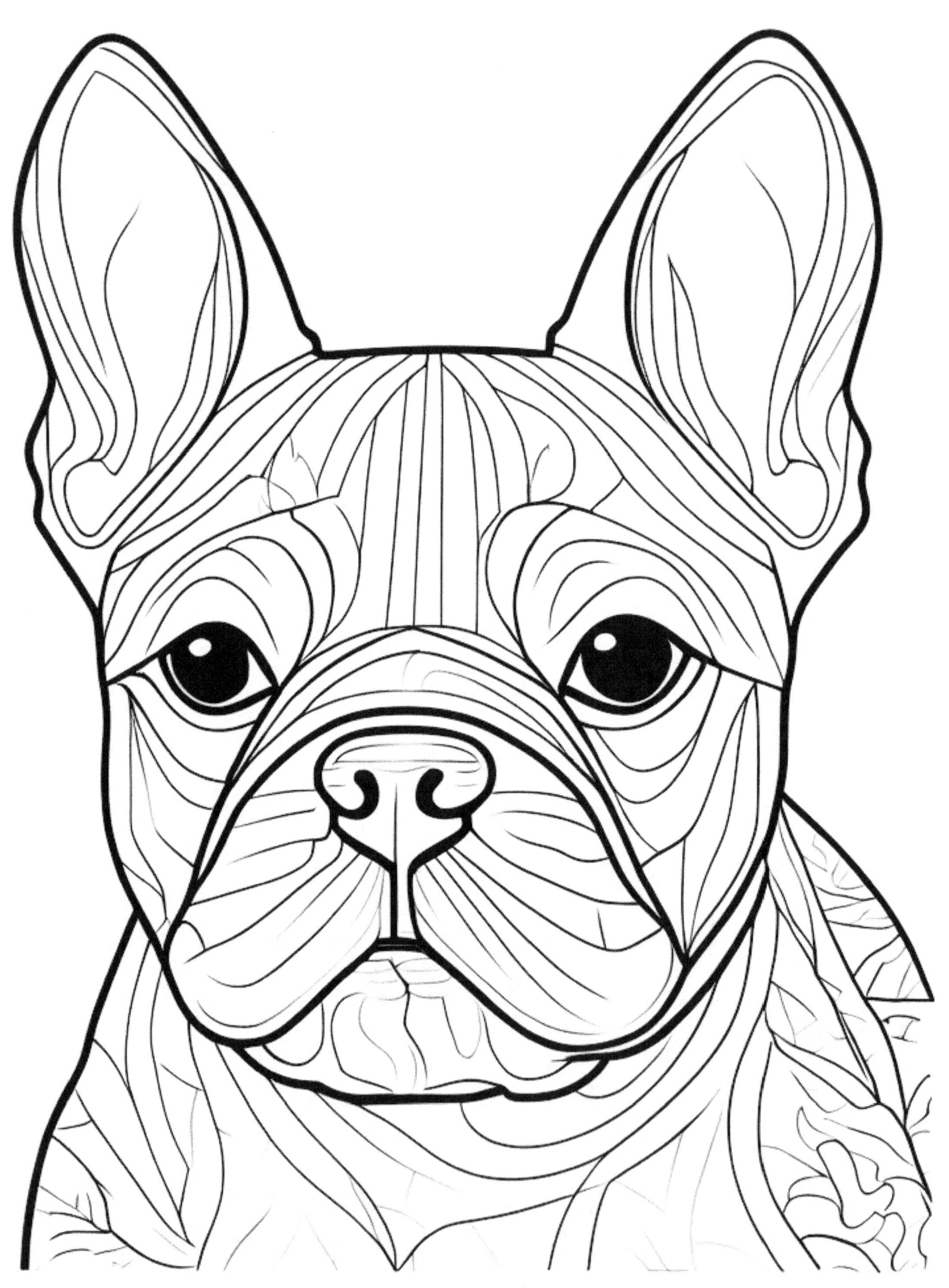

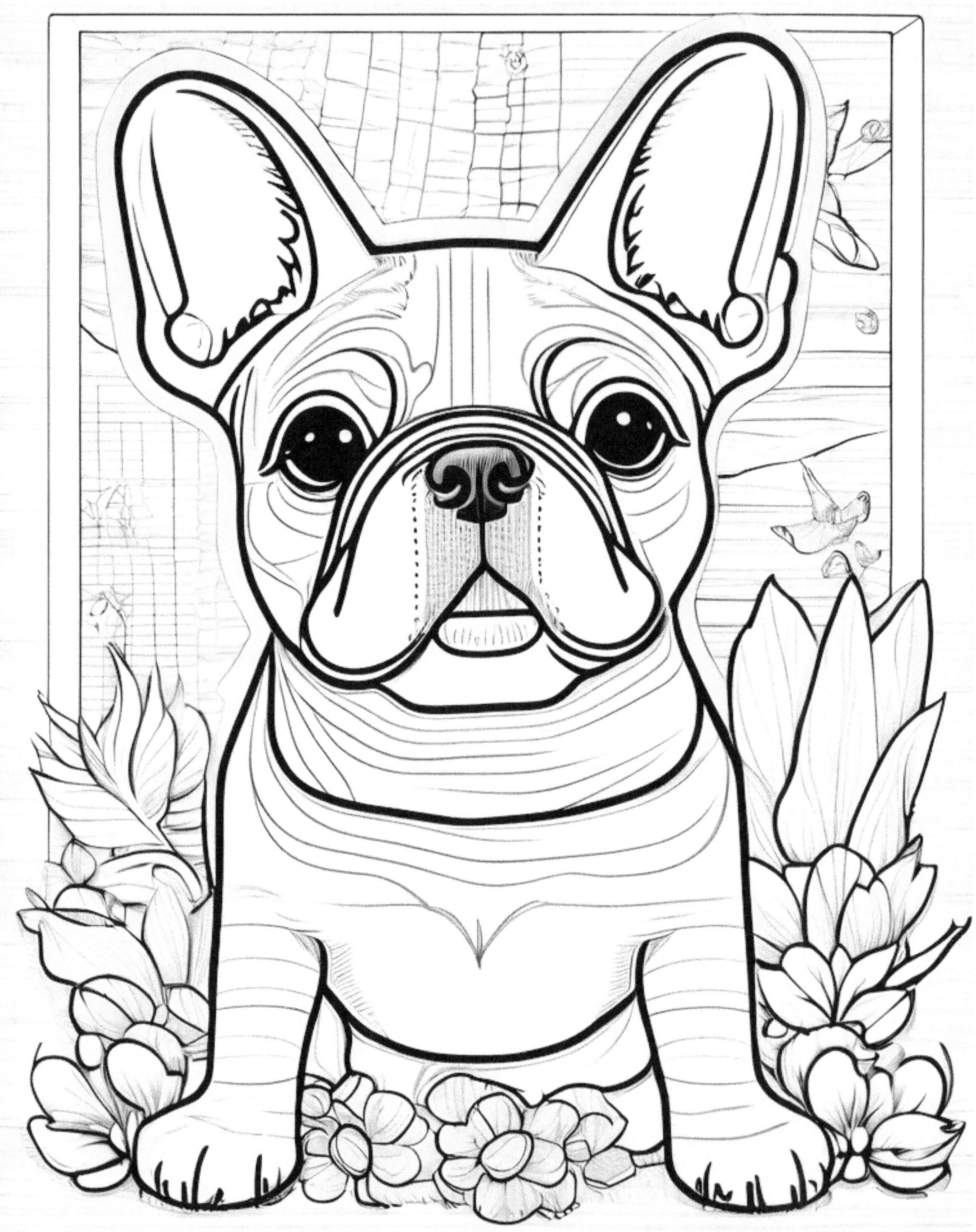

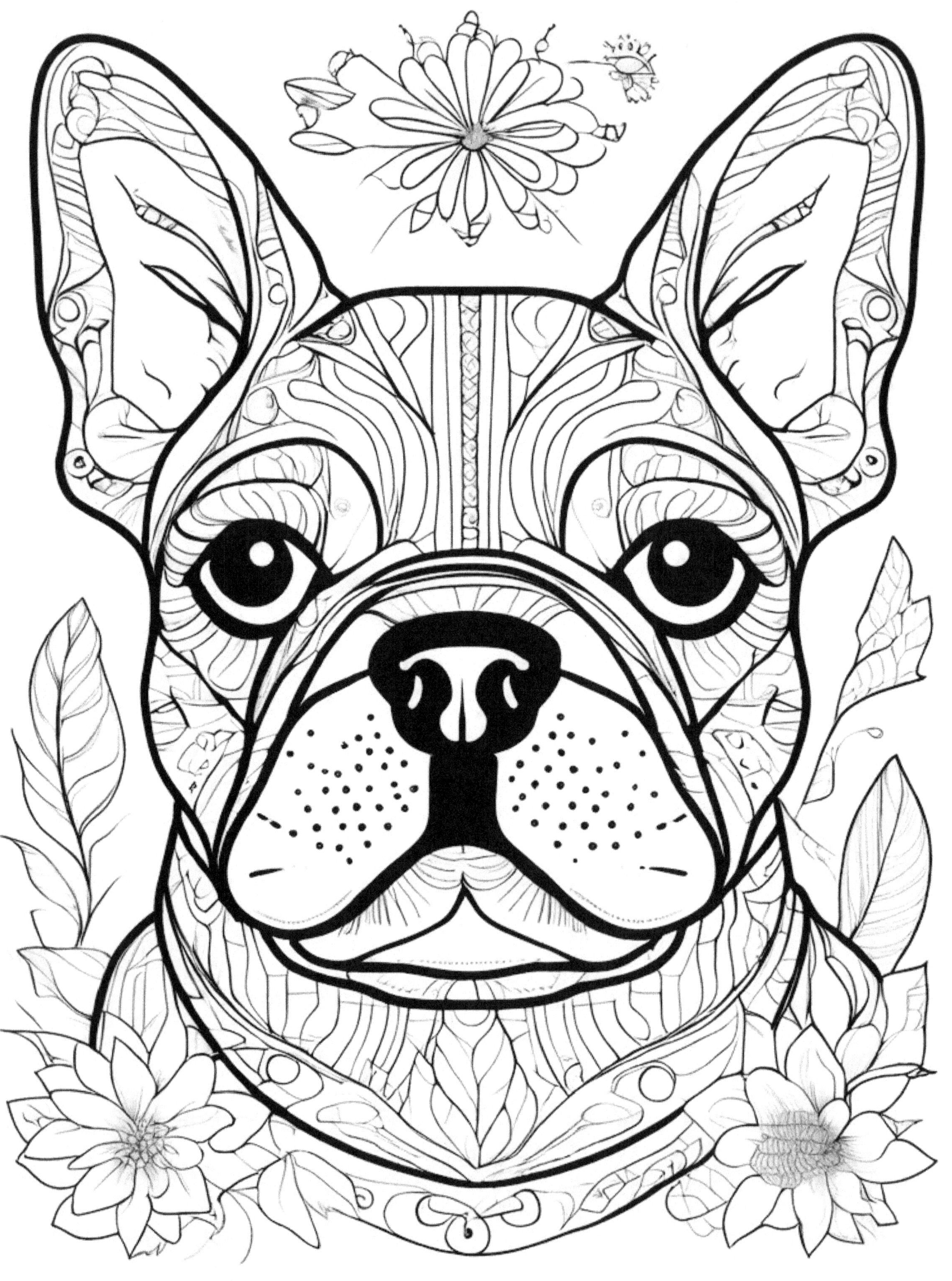

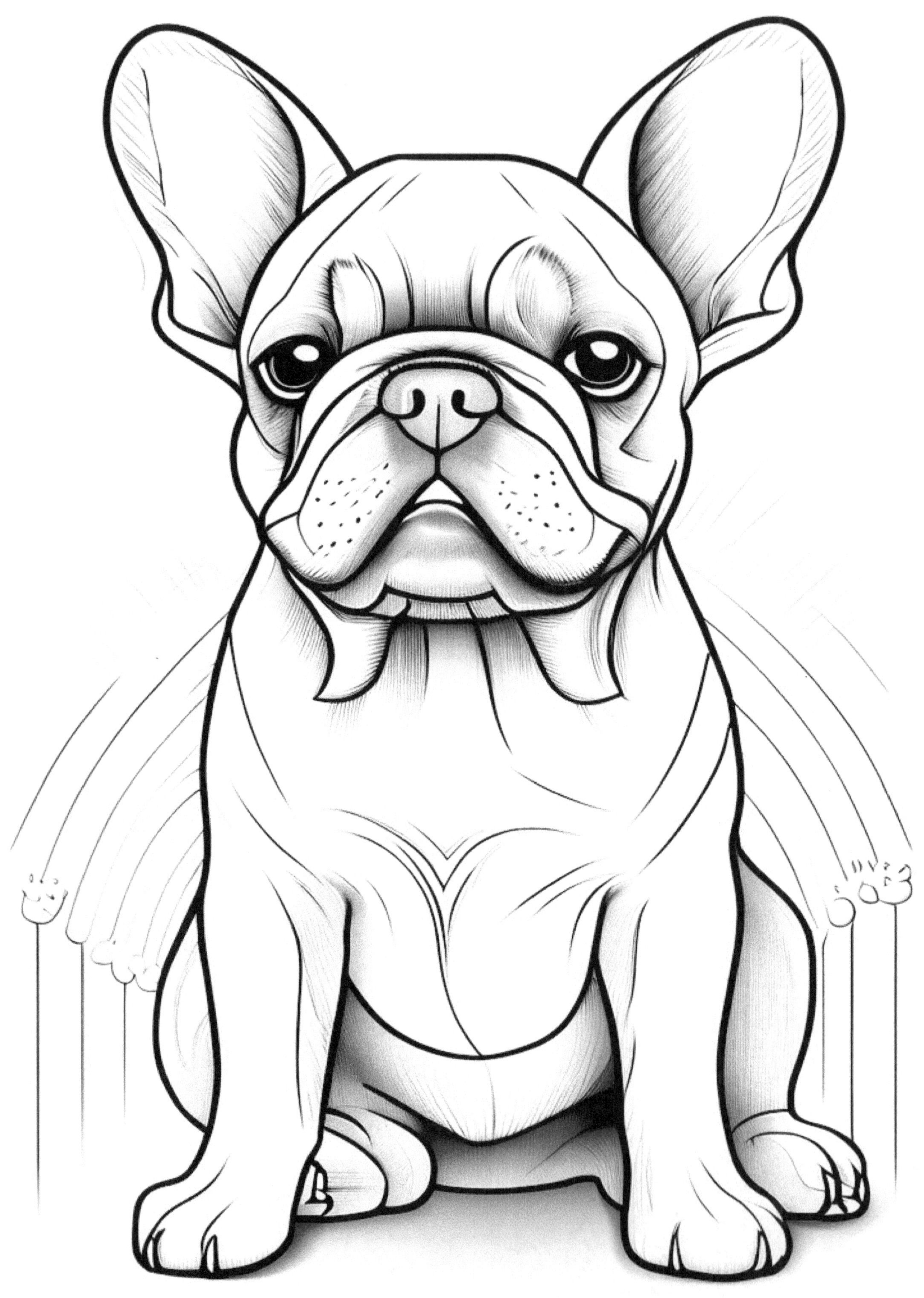

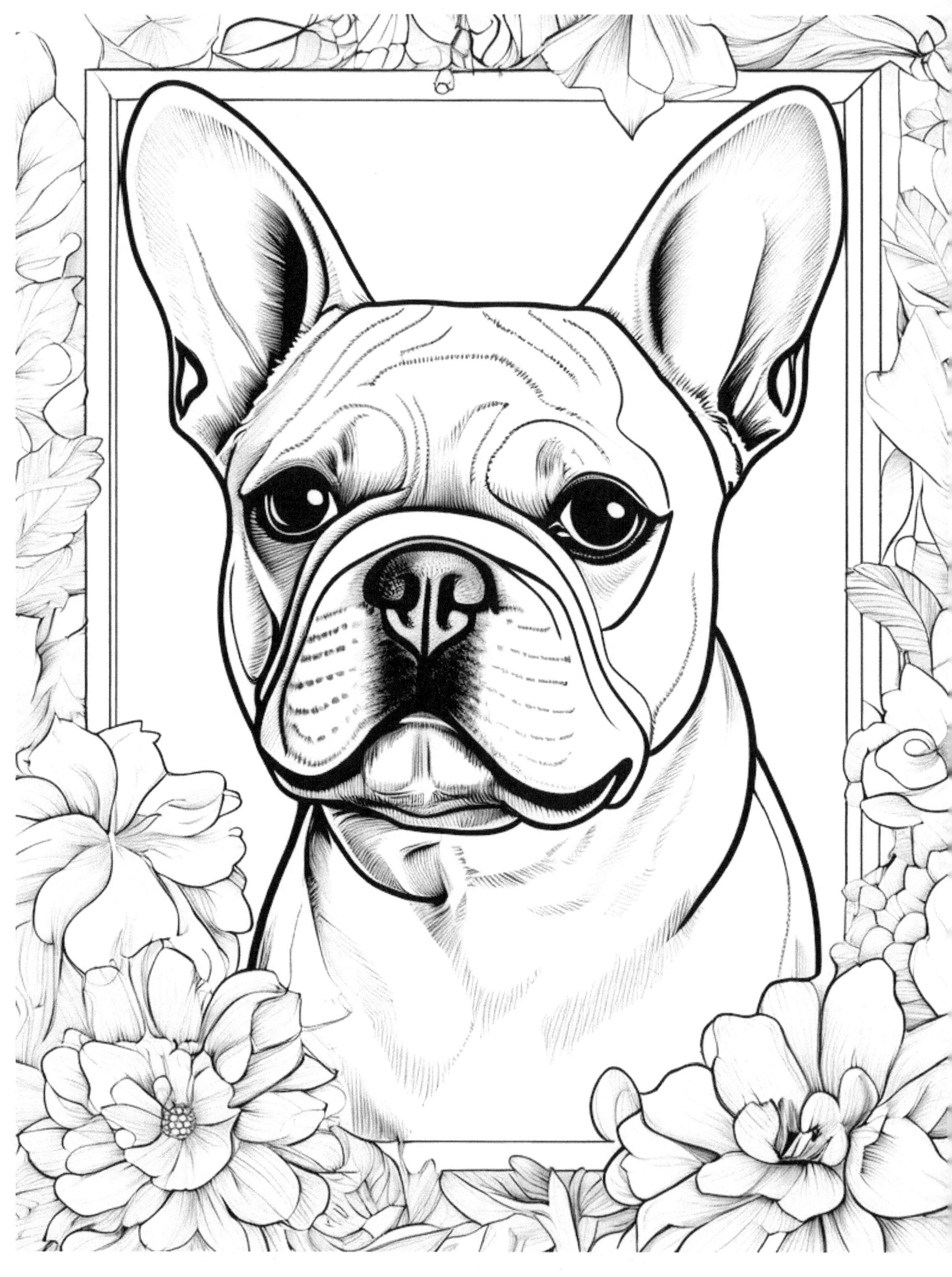

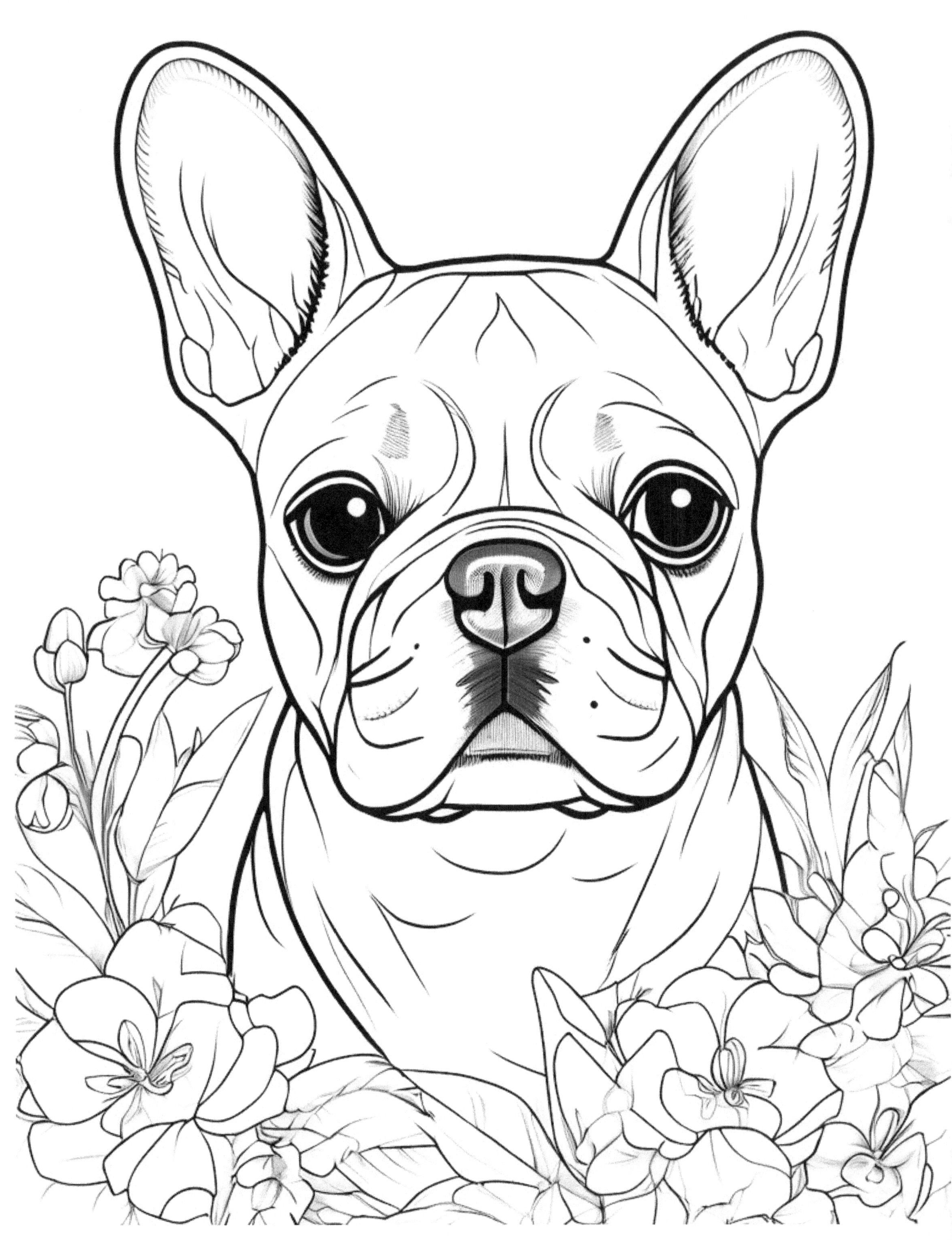

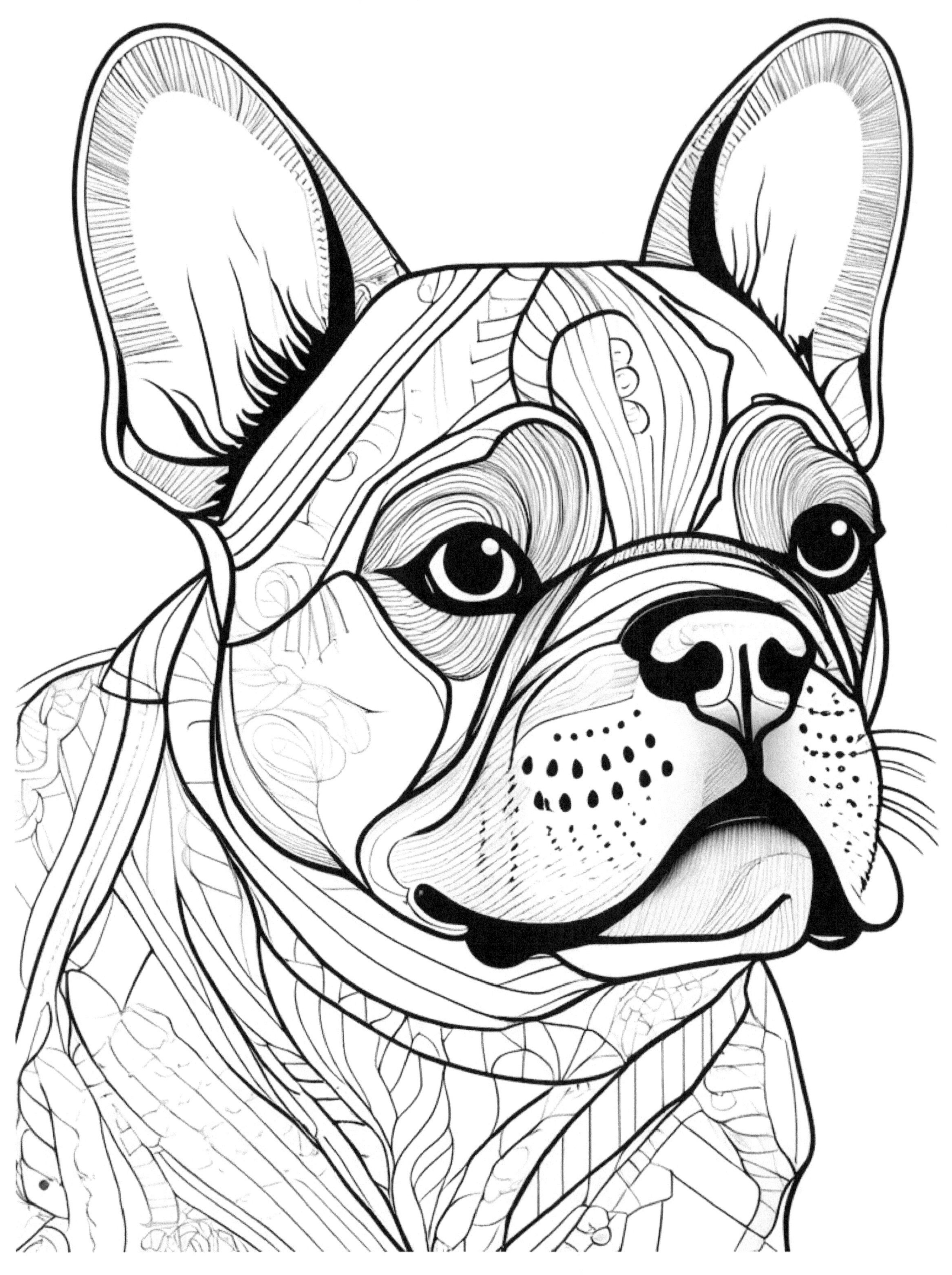

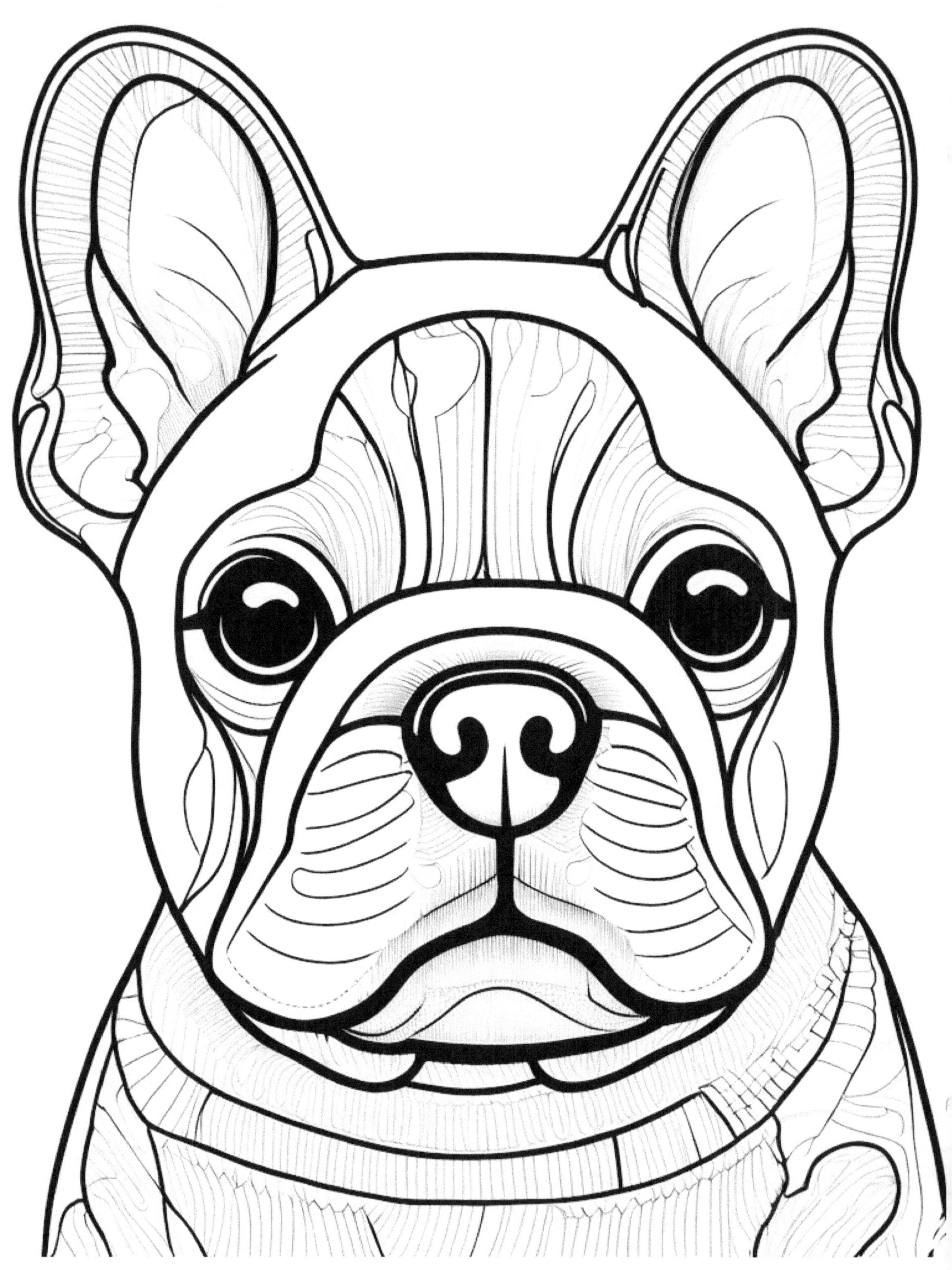

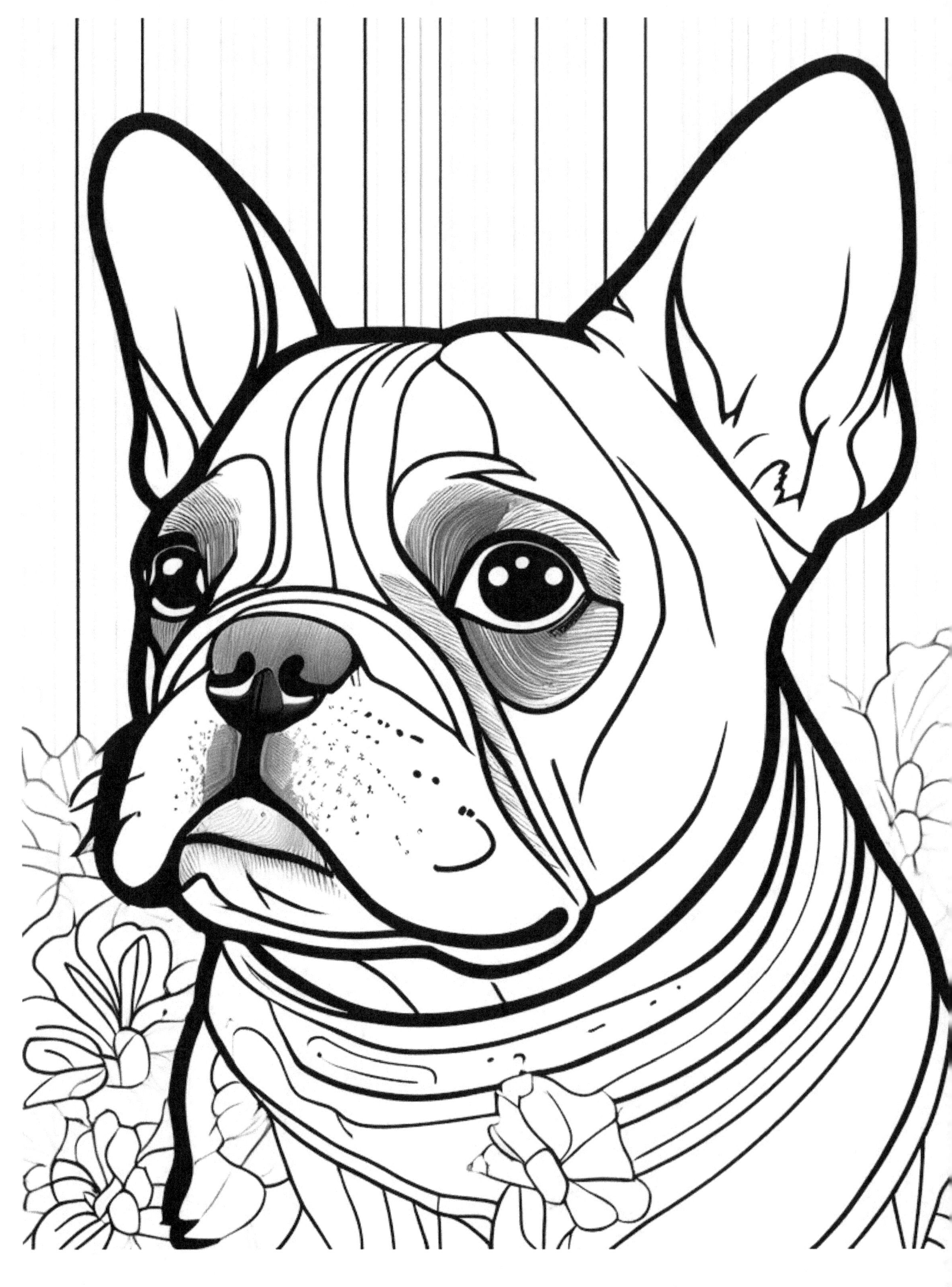

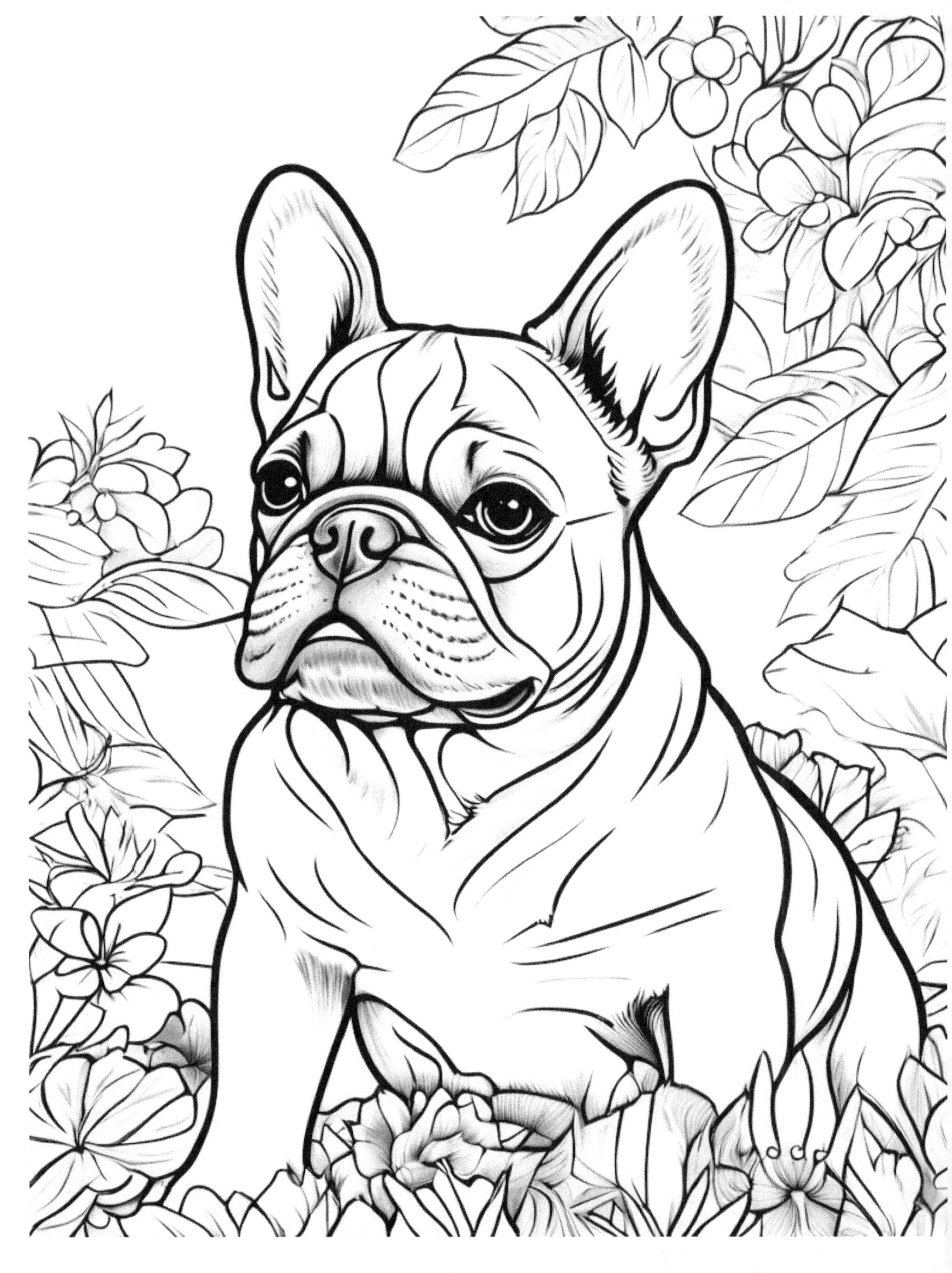

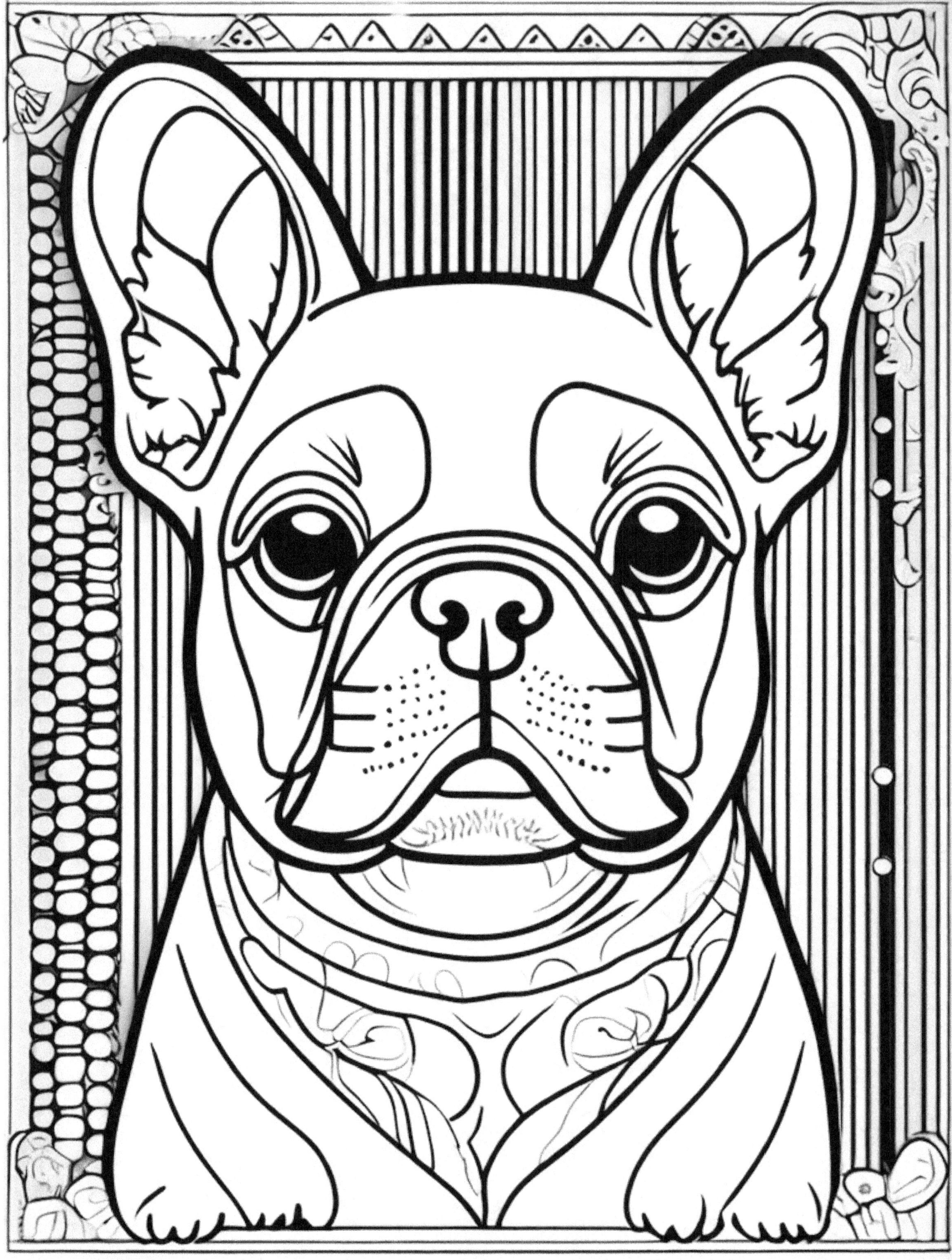

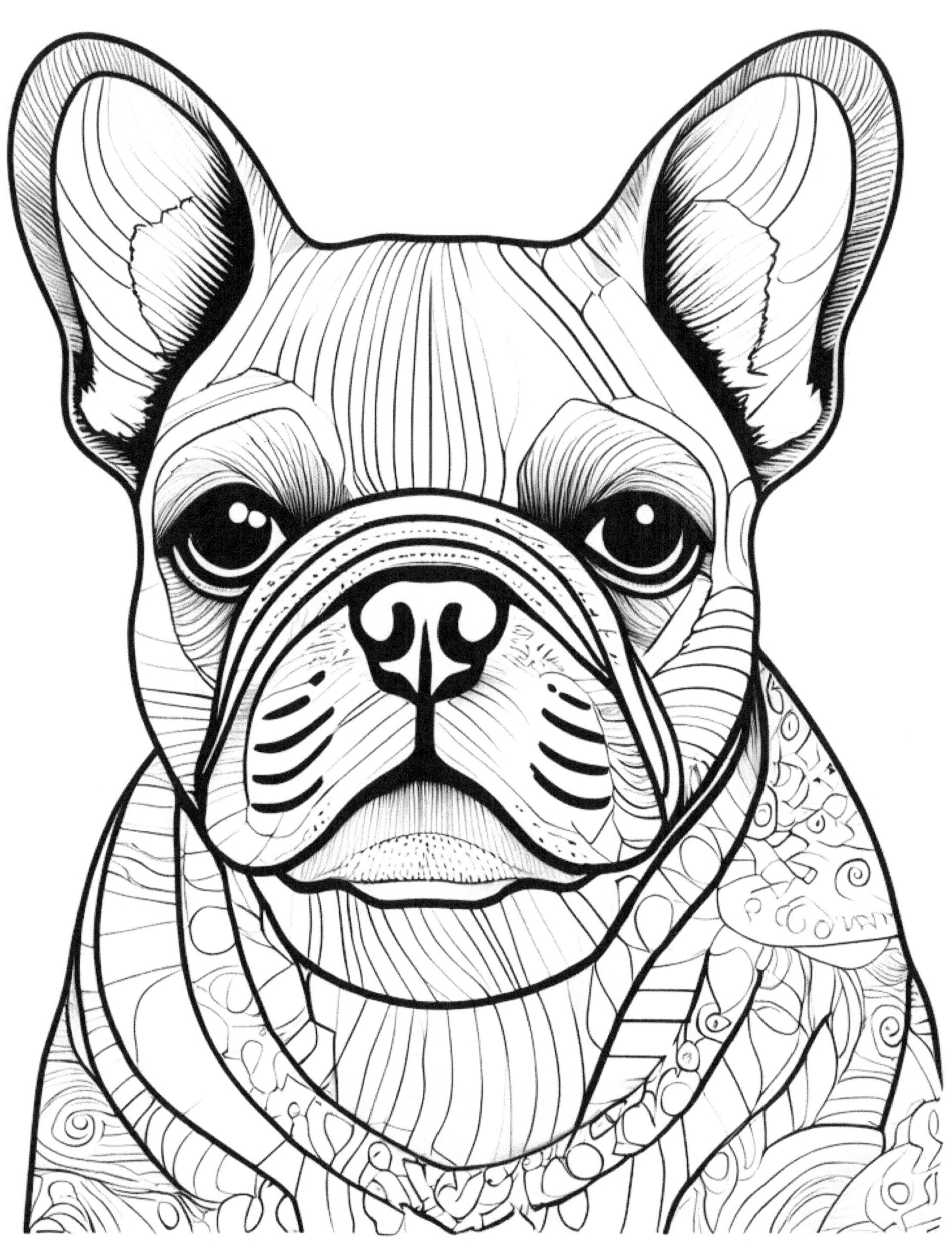

Just as a French bulldog brings comfort and joy to its owner, I hope this book has brought some happiness into your life.

May the memories created here remain vivid in your mind, bringing a smile to your face whenever you remember this time dedicated to the art of coloring.

May your journey continue full of vibrant colors and moments of inner peace.

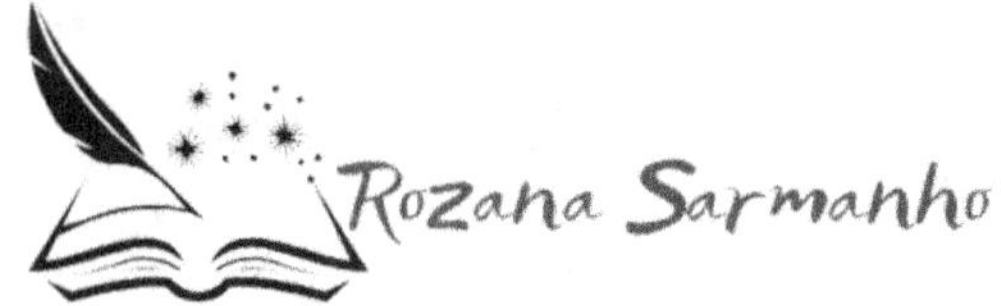